TWIST-and-TURN
BARGELLO
QUILTS

Eileen Wright

Martingale®
& COMPANY

Credits

President & CEO: Tom Wierzbicki
Editor in Chief: Mary V. Green
Managing Editor: Tina Cook
Developmental Editor: Karen Costello Soltys
Technical Editor: Nancy Mahoney
Copy Editor: Marcy Heffernan
Design Director: Stan Green
Production Manager: Regina Girard
Illustrator: Laurel Strand
Cover & Text Designer: Shelly Garrison
Photographer: Brent Kane

Mission Statement

Dedicated to providing quality products
and service to inspire creativity.

Twist-and-Turn Bargello Quilts
© 2009 by Eileen Wright

That Patchwork Place® is an imprint of
Martingale & Company®.

Martingale & Company
19021 120th Ave. NE, Suite 102
Bothell, WA 98011-9511 USA
ShopMartingale.com

Printed in China
17 16 15 14   13 12 11

**Library of Congress Cataloging-in-Publication Data
is available upon request.**

ISBN: 978-1-56477-943-4

DEDICATION

To Brenda Stengel, mentor, friend, and owner of Satin Moon Quilt Shop in Victoria, British Columbia, on beautiful Vancouver Island in Canada. Brenda's encouragement and support have always been the wind beneath my wings.

ACKNOWLEDGMENTS

No book ever reaches store shelves without the help of many people whose involvement in the author's life helps make her dream a reality. Many quilters have participated in my quilting journey and I am so very grateful to all of them.

My sincere thanks to Kaye Wood and Eleanor Burns, my very first television quilting teachers in the 1990s. Their television shows taught me everything that went into making my first few quilts.

And to Mary Wasley, my first local quilt teacher. Mary helped me to put a lifetime of dressmaking and a few months of television lessons into a new reality. She taught me a very high standard of piecing, which I cherish and practice to this day. Mary was also responsible for helping me get my first teaching assignment with a local quilt shop.

I owe a debt of gratitude to all of my quilting students, who have taught me so much and helped me improve my written instructions. I learn every time I teach.

A special thank-you to Pat Bays and Mary Laanela, awesome quilters, treasured friends, and eager pattern testers. Both Mary and Pat have always been there for me with a bit of advice, a suggestion, a word of encouragement, or a thumbs-down when it was what I needed to hear.

I am forever grateful to my long-arm quilters, Pat and Don Bays of Nanaimo, British Columbia, Canada, and Nadia Wilson of Port Hardy, British Columbia, Canada. Without their quilting expertise I would have a huge collection of tops! These quilters are talented and creative professionals who always make my work look better. I am so glad to have these people in my life.

Thank-you to everyone at Martingale & Company for putting my creative dreams into the reality of this book and to all the lovely quilters whose paths have crossed mine on this journey, to inspire me and bring joy to my life.

CONTENTS

INTRODUCTION ▪ 7

NECESSARY TOOLS ▪ 8

FABRICS FOR BARGELLO QUILTS ▪ 10

BUILDING STRIP SETS ▪ 14

THE PROJECTS

AURORA BOREALIS ▪ 18

ISLAND SUNSET ▪ 24

COSMIC TWIST ▪ 30

SUPERNOVA ▪ 36

QUALICUM ZEPHYR ▪ 44

INFINITY ▪ 50

NEBULA ▪ 58

SURF SONG ▪ 64

SURF SONG WALL HANGING ▪ 70

BARGELLO PLACE MATS ▪ 76

BARGELLO TABLE RUNNER ▪ 80

GALLERY OF QUILTS ▪ 84

FINISHING YOUR QUILT ▪ 89

ABOUT THE AUTHOR ▪ 96

INTRODUCTION

One of my earliest quilts that utilized rotary cutting and strip piecing was a basic bargello made in flannels, which were new to my local quilt shop. Later the shop owner suggested I was a sucker for punishment. I don't remember having any difficulty with the fabric or the quilt, nor do I remember having a specific pattern. I must have made some how-to notes from one of my television quilting classes. My memory is that it was all a very logical process.

I became interested in twisting and creating unusual designs with bargello-style quilts when I read an article in an Australian quilting magazine many years ago, complete with pictures of quilts by Chris Timmins. The quilts were obviously strip pieced—an efficient method that appealed to me from the very beginning of my quilting career. I don't believe that you can piece accurately and be fast—but you can be efficient. Strip piecing is *efficient*, and it's my favorite construction method. I've always preferred accurate and precise techniques over casual, less well-finished ones.

It's my hope that my quilts will be around and enjoyed long after I am gone. If they become a tattered and well-loved blanket 50 or 100 years from now, my mission will have been accomplished.

Beth Ann Williams's book, *Colorwash Bargello Quilts*, (Martingale and Company, 2001) has influenced my creative process a great deal. Although I haven't made any quilts from the book, it's in my library, and the pages have been studied with pleasure many times. I think all things seen and loved stay in our memory, where they simmer and stew, and then come forth at some future date as a new idea, if we simply let our mind work that way. I have always preferred creating original quilt designs, although I have supported huge numbers of designers by purchasing their books and patterns. Some day I might even get around to making some of these wonderful designs.

All of the bargello quilts in this book are made using regular strip-piecing techniques with a range of fabrics that produce a gradation of color in light to dark order as a rule. I prefer a color-wash effect in my fabric runs wherever possible, and that no doubt hails back to Beth Ann Williams's beautiful quilts. However, I always gravitate toward batiks and vibrant colors.

Assigning numbers to the fabrics and then following a number chart or "paint by number" map allows the fabrics to be rearranged out of numerical sequence so that the design changes shape and direction. The fabrics wiggle and twist to form an exciting new design or secondary image. Varying widths of slices helps produce rounder curves as well as sharper points.

This technique allows you to utilize precise skills and basic quilting techniques to create unusual, artistic shapes and designs in a relatively easy manner. If you can map the design in numbers, then it can be created in fabric. While quilters will develop their own favorite methods and techniques, I believe that accuracy and good techniques will accomplish a better-looking, longer-lasting quilt every time and make the quilting easier, too. In this book, I share the methods that work best for me. I encourage each of you to use what you like and create your own best methods along the way. There's always more than one way to go about making a quilt. Enjoy the journey!

NECESSARY TOOLS

Good work requires good equipment. Ask any carpenter. At a minimum, you'll need a sewing machine in good working order with a ¼" patchwork foot. If you're a master of your machine, the process of creating a quilt or any stitched item will be that much easier.

CUTTING TOOLS

You'll need a self-healing cutting mat, a clear acrylic ruler, and a rotary cutter. Extra mats and rulers are nice to have on hand if you are a prolific quilter. You'll also need a cutting table or station. In fact, some of the projects in this book are much easier to create if you are able to set up two cutting stations for the duration of the project.

A cutting mat at least 24" x 36" works well for all of the quilts in this book, as the fabric slices for some quilts can be rather long. And if you have two mats, it's easier to keep the multiple strip sets organized while working on your quilt.

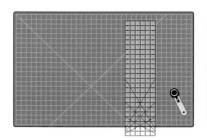

A rotary cutter with a sharp blade is essential. A dull blade pushes the fabric threads into the cutting mat, creating extra fraying along the edges of your cut strips. You can avoid this aggravation by inserting a new blade in your cutter before you start your quilt.

My personal preference for rulers is an 8½" x 24" lime green Omnigrip ruler by Omnigrid. The Omnigrip rulers grip the fabric just a little, and you can cut a strip of fabric in one swipe without walking your fingers up the ruler, as long as you exert good pressure in the middle of the ruler. To make that easier I recommend The Original Gypsy Gripper ruler handle. I'm not a gadget person, but because I have arthritis in my hands, I thought this tool might make cutting easier, and it does. One grip with pressure makes the slice very fast. Getting the cutting done faster is a bonus in my opinion.

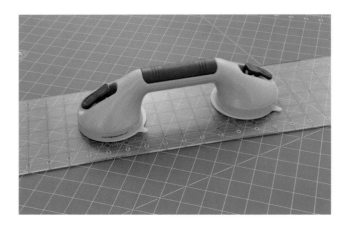

PRESSING EQUIPMENT

Because pressing is so important to the finished results of any project, you will also need a good solid ironing board without a lot of padding. If you have a handy carpenter-type person in your life, you might wish to have him or her make a larger pressing surface to fit on top of your regular ironing board. You'll need a piece of plywood cut to the size of rectangle you want, making it slightly larger than your ironing board. On the underneath side of the plywood, use 1" x 1" wood strips along the edges of the plywood to frame the rectangle and secure it to your ironing board. Cover the top of the plywood with one or two layers of cotton batting and a single layer of muslin, wrapped to the back edge and stapled firmly in place. I prefer a very hard ironing board rather than one with a lot of padding. This type of firm surface, combined with a good-quality steam iron, makes easy work of pressing the many seam allowances in a bargello quilt.

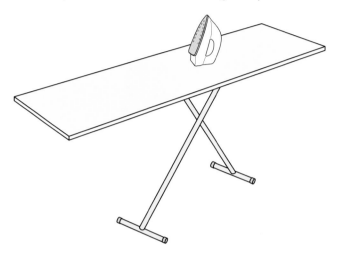

NEEDLES AND THREADS

Always match your sewing machine thread to your fabric content. Since we make quilts using 100%-cotton fabrics, a 50-weight 100%-cotton thread works best for strip piecing. I like Mettler Silk Finish thread in medium gray, as it blends quite nicely with the wide variety of colors used in a bargello quilt. I only change my thread color if I'm sewing on stark white or black fabrics. Similarly, you need a needle size that works with the thread weight and fabric you are using. A Sharp 80/12 needle does the job nicely.

BATTING

When it comes to quilt batting, most quilters eventually find a favorite. I have tried a few varieties, including wool and the newer bamboo products, but my personal favorite is a bleached 80/20 cotton/polyester blend because it's lightweight, has a lovely loft, and drapes nicely. To me, it looks the best when quilted and is cozy and comfortable to sleep under. If you prefer a polyester batting, be sure to choose one that has been heat bonded rather than chemically bonded, for safety, and is guaranteed not to beard through your cotton fabrics.

MISCELLANEOUS SUPPLIES

You will also need basic sewing accessories: scissors, thread snips, straight pins, chalk markers, a seam ripper, quilters' safety pins in large quantity, masking tape, and decorative quilting threads at a minimum. I also find a stiletto or awl handy to use when joining the rows, but a seam ripper can be used in a pinch.

In addition, you may wish to own a Ruby Beholder® and a green value finder as well, for sorting your fabrics into light to dark sequences. Quilt shops often have these on hand for your use while shopping.

The gadget lovers among you will no doubt add to the list of basic supplies.

FABRICS FOR BARGELLO QUILTS

Choosing fabrics for any new project is the most exciting part for me—aside from seeing the quilt finished.

FABRIC SELECTION

Don't be intimidated when you read that you'll need 20 fabrics to make a project (or 24 fabrics for "Surf Song" on page 64). There are many ways to reach the desired collection of 20 or more fabrics. First you need to decide what color or theme you want to incorporate into your vision of the chosen design. Don't feel that you need to replicate my fabric selections; that would be difficult since some of the fabrics have been in my stash for a few years.

You can either decide on one or two colors and pull out every possible fabric from your own stash or go to your favorite quilt shop and see what inspires you from the fabric selection currently available. Even if you choose the second option, I encourage you to use as many fabrics as possible from your stash. You bought the fabrics because you liked them, and using them is guaranteed to give you a very self-righteous feeling. Not to mention you'll have an excuse to replenish your stash.

For best results, choose your fabrics carefully. The project instructions tell you how many fabrics you'll need from each color group you've selected. I recommend you amass more fabrics than you'll need for the project, and then eliminate the ones that aren't blending with the other fabrics. The fabrics should range from light to dark within each color group. You'll want to include fabrics in a variety of scales and textures, plus a zinger or two; this will add sparkle and movement to your quilt.

In "Aurora Borealis," I used two color groups and various prints to create the look I wanted (see page 18 for the full quilt).

My only advice on choosing fabrics is never allow yourself to be talked into using a fabric that you really don't like, especially if it will be in a prominent position in your quilt. That said, do keep an open mind to fabrics that seem to fit but are just a bit unusual or out of your usual comfort zone. The inclusion of one or two fabrics that fit that description will probably be the ones that make your quilt sing. Always be on the lookout for a few of these fabrics, which I call zingers. I've included two examples of zinger fabrics on the facing page. They are really important for a great result, providing they blend with the overall fabric lineup.

Fabric 5 from "Cosmic Twist" on page 30.

Fabric 10 from "Island Sunset" on page 24.

I admit I usually end up with a collection of 40 or so fabrics before I actually choose the "perfect" 20. Even then, when the quilt is finished, I may have second thoughts about my selection. While I agonize over this process far too much, I urge you to try not to!

I encourage you to trust your instincts and create your own vision of any of these designs. To illustrate why, I need to tell you a little story about my dear friend and pattern tester, Mary Laanela. When she first saw my "Surf Song Wall Hanging" (page 70), she loved it, but immediately said she would like to make it in florals so that it would look like a field of wild flowers growing and rippling in the breeze on the side of a mountain. Her vision, which she named "Floral Melody" is on page 87. Mary's verbal idea inspired me to create a second quilt using the same design, which I called "Wind Song" (page 87).

I believe we all inspire each other along our quilting journey. Let your own creativity blossom with these quilts. There are no rules when it comes to the fabrics you use in your quilts. You need only please yourself.

ORGANIZING FABRICS BY VALUE

Once you've accumulated a large selection of fabrics in one or two colors, sort them in a stack of lights to darks for a one-color quilt or in a light-to-dark stack for each color group for a two-color quilt. When using two color groups in your quilt, an uneven split of the colors is usually more visually appealing. Ultimately you'll want 8 or 9 fabrics of one color and 11 or 12 of the second color. (The total number of fabrics you'll need in each color group is included in the project instructions.)

Your sorted stack of fabrics doesn't have to include fabrics that are very light or even very dark. Value is relative, so just think of arranging the fabrics you're working with in order from the lightest to the darkest value. Sorting by value can be fairly easy in most cases. But it can be difficult to determine the value of a print or batik that has various colors or values or is a high-contrast print (dark motifs on light background, for instance).

One helpful tool for assessing value is a Ruby Beholder. This dark red plastic tool can be used to view the relative value in fabric. When you look at your fabrics through the plastic, the colors disappear and you are left looking at shades of light to dark. However, this tool doesn't work with red-toned fabrics. Instead, try using a green value finder. It takes some practice, but using these tools can give you a real sense of the value of your fabrics.

Another way to determine the value of a fabric is to arrange your fabrics in sequence from light to dark, with about 1" of each fabric showing. Then photocopy the fabrics in black and white. The resulting image in shades of gray can help you easily see if you need to rearrange any of them to get the correct light-to-dark order. Sometimes standing back and squinting at the pile of fabrics will work for testing value, too.

Fabrics range from light to dark in "Supernova."
For a full view of this quilt, see page 36.

If you are still uncertain about the value of your fabrics, seek the assistance of a quilt-shop employee. If you're purchasing all the fabrics for a project, one of the staff members would probably enjoy helping you make your selections. Even if you're starting with fabrics from your stash and planning to add to it, I'm sure they won't mind helping you. They usually share our addiction to fabric and understand that quilters collect fabric and need to use fabrics from their stash from time to time.

Once you have determined the correct order of your fabric lineup, take a digital picture or label the fabrics in some way, especially if you still have to wash them. You can even write the sequence number in pencil in the selvage if needed.

Strive for Even Gradation

I find that a fairly even gradation of value from one fabric to the next will produce the most pleasing results. I prefer a smooth blend of values rather than a striped look. But any time you use more than one color, you are probably going to get some striping. Blue and green are about the only colors that blend beautifully from light to dark. For some reason green is near the bottom on my list of favorite colors. And in "Surf Song" (page 64), I actually wanted multiple "waves" or stripes in the blues. For the most part, trust your own instincts about color.

PREPARING YOUR FABRICS

To wash or not to wash fabrics is a subject of much debate and personal choice. I don't believe I can change the mind of anyone who doesn't prewash their fabrics. Personally, every fabric that comes into my home goes directly to the laundry closet to be soaked in cold water, spun, and dried in a hot dryer.

If I have any concerns about the color running, then I set the color with a product called Retayne, which is available at most quilt shops. Just follow the directions on the bottle.

When your fabric comes out of the dryer, fold it in half lengthwise, matching the selvages and making sure there are no twists or wrinkles along the fold. Press the fabric while it's folded in half, being careful not to press over the fold line, only up to it. If you press the fold you will probably never be able to remove the crease. Once your fabric is folded on grain and well pressed, it is ready to be cut into the required strips for your project.

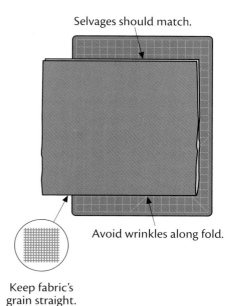

Selvages should match.

Keep fabric's grain straight.

Avoid wrinkles along fold.

CUTTING STRAIGHT STRIPS

Cutting strips at an exact right angle to the folded edge of your fabric is essential for making accurate strip sets. If your mat can fit 42"-wide fabric folded just once, leave it folded just once. The more folds you make, the greater chance that you'll end up with crooked strips.

Crooked strip

Place your pressed fabric on your cutting mat with the folded edge nearest to your body. Place the ruler on top of the fabric along the right edge, aligning a line of the ruler with the fabric fold. The raw, uneven edges should extend beyond the ruler's edge, as shown above right. Cut along the long edge of the ruler to trim off the end of the fabric, making a straight edge. This is known as a cleanup cut. (Reverse this procedure if you are left-handed.) Save the little bit of fabric removed by the cleanup cut; this nice snippet can be used to create the fabric map required for your project. See "Creating a Fabric Map" at right.

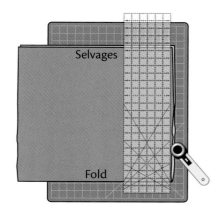

Selvages

Fold

Now carefully turn the fabric over, placing the straightened edge to your left and the fold at the bottom. Cut strips in the width specified in the project instructions, measuring from the straight edge. For example, if you need 2"-wide strips, place the 2" line on the ruler on the straightened edge of the fabric and cut along the ruler's right edge.

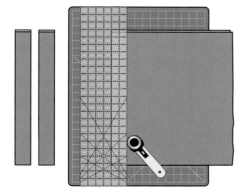

CREATING A FABRIC MAP

You will need a snippet of each bargello fabric, arranged in light-to-dark order, with assigned numbers. Tape or glue the snippets to a sheet of white paper in numerical sequence and write the corresponding number above each fabric. This is your fabric map, and it's critical to the successful completion of all of the projects in this book.

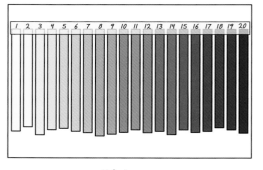

Fabric map

BUILDING STRIP SETS

Bargello quilts are made by cutting varying widths of fabric strips, sewing the strips together in predetermined sequences to create strip sets (also called "strata"), and then cutting the strip sets into slices. Sometimes you'll take a slice apart at a seam line to make segments. When the slices and/or segments are sewn together, the beauty of the undulating pattern emerges. But it all starts with building the strip sets.

1. Cut the number of fabric strips, in the required width, from each designated fabric for the project you are making.

Sewing Accurate Strip Sets

Precisely sewn strip sets are the foundation for making bargello quilts. A straight, scant ¼"-wide seam allowance is used for all of the projects in this book.

Use a shorter-than-normal stitch length of 13 or 14 stitches per inch. This is approximately 2.0 on a sewing machine that has a stitch-length range of 0–5. A shorter stitch length will prevent the seams on the cut slices from opening as you work with them.

To check the accuracy of your seam allowance, cut three strips of fabric, each 1½" x 5", and using a ¼"-wide seam allowance, sew them together along their long edges. Press and measure the center strip on the right side of the three-strip unit. The center strip should measure exactly 1" between the seams. If your seam allowances are wider than ¼", the finished project will be smaller than the size stated. Accurate ¼" seam allowances are especially important with bargello quilts that have so many seams.

2. Lay out the fabric strips in stacks, one for each fabric, in the order in which they will be sewn. Fabric 1 will be on the left and fabric 20 on the right as shown. You'll be sewing strips together in pairs with the even-numbered strip on top.

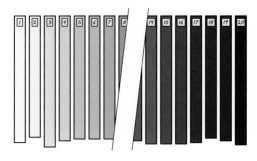

3. Lay a fabric 2 strip on top of a fabric 1 strip, right sides together and raw edges aligned. Sew the strips together along their long right-hand edge using a scant ¼"-wide seam allowance.

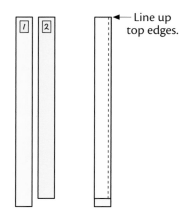

4. Continue sewing fabric 1 and fabric 2 strips in pairs. To avoid distortions and save thread, you may want to chain piece the strips. Begin stitching on a small scrap of fabric and sew to its edge. Then feed a pair of strips under the presser foot and continue sewing. Don't cut the thread between pairs; just keep running the strips through your

sewing machine. As you finish sewing the last pair, sew onto another fabric scrap, and then clip the threads between the sewn pieces. Refer to "Pressing Direction" on page 16 and press the seam allowances in the direction indicated in the project illustrations.

5. Lay a fabric 4 strip on top of a fabric 3 strip. Sew the strips together in pairs along their long right-hand edges, in the same manner as before.

6. Continue in the same manner, sewing the strips in pairs, making sure the even-numbered strip is always on top. Sewing the strips in pairs (and pressing) before joining all the strips together helps prevent the finished strip set from becoming bowed (or curved).

7. Sew the strip pairs together in the order in which they're numbered. Always flip the higher number over onto the lower number, right sides together, and sew down the right-hand edge. Continue joining the strips until they are all sewn into one complete strip set.

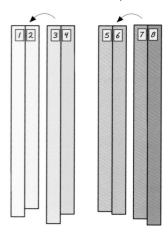

Sew strip pairs together.

8. Build the number of strips sets in the correct numerical sequence as indicated in the instructions for your project. Note that for some of the projects, you'll need more strip sets of some fabrics than others. In these cases, you'll be instructed to build extra strip sets using only a partial lineup of the fabrics.

PREVENTING STRIP SETS FROM BOWING

Bowing is a common problem when creating strip sets. Reversing the sewing direction will help prevent this.

Sew the strips in pairs as instructed in "Building Strip Sets" and press the seam allowances in the direction indicated in the project instructions. To maximize the number of slices you can cut, you'll want to keep the strips even on one end of the completed strip set. To do this and still prevent the strip set from bowing, start by arranging the strip pairs in the correct sequence and line up the end you are keeping even. When sewing the strip pairs together, flip the pairs over and sew from the uneven end.

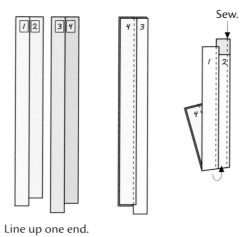

Line up one end.

After sewing the first two strips together, you'll be sewing from the uneven end until all strip pairs are sewn into a single strip set.

One at a Time

If the process of making multiple strip sets confuses you, it's totally acceptable to sew and press one complete strip set at a time. Always work within your own comfort level.

PRESSING DIRECTION

For many projects you'll make a specified number of identical strip sets. Some projects require that half of the strip-set seam allowances be pressed toward the lowest fabric number and the remaining strip-set seam allowances be pressed toward the highest fabric number. Other projects require that all seam allowances be pressed toward the even-numbered strips.

Pressing the seam allowances in the correct direction is critical in order to accurately match seam lines, and the direction has been carefully thought out ahead of time. Press the strip pairs in the direction indicated in the instructions for the project you're making; this way the seam allowances will oppose each other and neatly butt against each other (or nest) when you are sewing the rows together. Then, with a bit of practice you'll be able to wiggle the seam intersections into a perfect match and stitch without using pins. Honest.

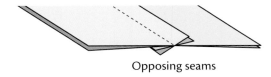

Opposing seams

PRESSING STRIPS

I like to use steam for pressing strips, as it helps set the seam firmly in place.

1. Press each stack of matching strip pairs immediately after stitching, before sewing the next stack of strips. Lay the strip set on the ironing board with the seam allowances away from your body. The fabric on top is the one the seam allowances will be pressed toward. For example, for strip pairs of fabrics 1 and 2, if you want the seam allowances pressed toward the smaller fabric number (1), make sure fabric 1 is on top. Similarly, if you want the seam allowances pressed toward the higher number, position the pair with fabric 2 on top.

2. Position the strips along the length of your ironing board, with the line of stitching as straight as possible. Press the seam flat from the wrong side to set the stitches and remove any puckers.

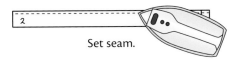

Set seam.

3. Flip the top piece over, right side up, and run your finger along the seam line ahead of the iron. Use the side of the iron to gently push the top fabric strip over the seam allowances, making sure there are no tucks in the fabric as you press the seam to one side. Do not wiggle the iron back and forth. Instead, hold it in place for a couple of seconds to firmly press the seam. Work your way along the entire strip in this manner.

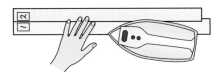

Push fabric away from seam
with side of iron.

4. Make sure the unit is lying straight on the board and once more press the strip pair along the seam line from the right side.

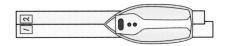

CUTTING SLICES

For projects with strip sets that are not identical or identical strip sets with seam allowances that are pressed in opposite directions, cutting is easier if you can set up two cutting stations. You'll find this helps keep the strip sets organized while you're working on your quilt.

For those projects where half of the strip sets have seam allowances pressed toward the lowest fabric number and the other half pressed toward the highest fabric number, place a sticky note with an arrow at the top of each cutting mat indicating which direction the seam allowances are pressed (up or down). Then position the strip sets on the appropriate mat with the seam allowances going in the same direction as the arrow. This will make it easier to alternately cut slices from the correct strip set as instructed for your project.

1. Fold a strip set in half *wrong side out* along the center seam line. Lay it on your cutting mat as shown below, making sure that all of the seams are straight, smooth, and parallel. Nest the seam allowances of each row, and then pin the top raw edges together using about four straight pins across the 42" width.

2. Trim the selvages on the right, uneven end of the strip set by carefully aligning a horizontal line of the cutting ruler with one of the strip set's internal seam lines. Be sure to remove any pins that lie under or near your ruler before cutting.

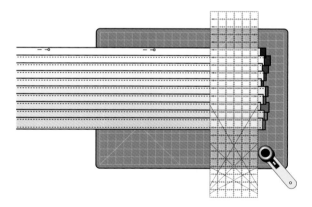

3. Place the straightened end on the left, align the desired measurement on your cutting ruler with the straightened end, and cut. Cut the number of slices required in the width indicated for each row of your project. If your ruler is shorter than the width of your folded strip set, slide your ruler the distance needed, keeping the edge of the ruler even with the cut edge, and continue cutting.

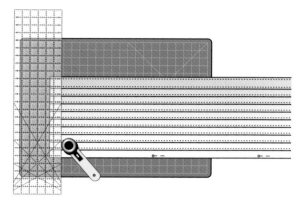

Cut slices.

Good Beginnings

If bargello techniques are new to you, on pages 64–83 you'll find four projects that use a basic bargello technique of sewing fabric strips together to make a loop. In this method, all of the fabrics stay in the original numerical sequence as determined by your fabric map. In the other seven projects, the fabric strips in the cut slices are rearranged out of numerical sequence to create the twisting designs.

AURORA BOREALIS

Aurora Borealis was my first personally acceptable finished twisted bargello quilt. I made many prototypes—one of which I sold on consignment in a local quilt shop—before I reached this stage. The shop's pattern buyer called to ask where I got the pattern, which led to me selling patterns and eventually teaching at the shop. The rest, as they say, is history. This quilt marked the beginning of a fun twisted journey for me.

CHOOSING FABRIC

This quilt uses 20 fabrics in two color groups: 9 in lighter or brighter colors and 11 in a coordinating color group. Fabrics in each color group should range from light to dark. I recommend you wait until the bargello center is finished to choose fabric for the border, because fabrics can take on a new life when they are sewn together. I suggest a dark fabric that enhances the overall appearance of your project and frames it nicely, plus a bright border accent. The border should enhance the total appearance of the quilt as well as frame it.

MATERIALS

Yardage is based on 42"-wide fabric.

¼ yard *each* of 11 coordinating bargello fabrics

¼ yard *each* of 9 lighter/brighter bargello fabrics

1½ yards of a dark fabric for borders and binding

¼ yard of a bright fabric for border accent

3¼ yards of fabric for backing

49" x 66" piece of batting

CUTTING

From *each* of the 20 bargello fabrics, cut:
4 strips, 1½" x 42"

From the dark fabric for borders and binding, cut:
7 outer-border strips, 3½" x 42"
6 binding strips, 2¼" x 42"
6 inner-border strips, 1½" x 42"

From the bright fabric for border accent, cut:
6 strips, 1" x 42"

Finished Size: 41¼" x 57½" ▪ Pieced and machine quilted by author

FABRIC MAP

Referring to page 13, use a scrap of each bargello fabric to create a fabric map. You'll need to refer to your map throughout the project in order to position all of the strips correctly to make the design shown.

MAKING THE STRIP SETS

Referring to "Building Strip Sets" on page 14 and using the 1½"-wide bargello fabric strips, sew the strips together in numerical order according to your fabric map to make four identical strip sets. On two strip sets, press the seam allowances *up*, toward fabric

On the remaining two strip sets, press the seam allowances *down*, toward fabric 20. Cut all odd-number rows from the strip sets with the seam allowances pressed up and all even-number rows from the strip sets with the seam allowances pressed down.

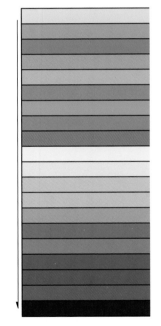

| Fabric 1 |
| Fabric 2 |
| Fabric 3 |
| Fabric 4 |
| Fabric 5 |
| Fabric 6 |
| Fabric 7 |
| Fabric 8 |
| Fabric 9 |
| Fabric 10 |
| Fabric 11 |
| Fabric 12 |
| Fabric 13 |
| Fabric 14 |
| Fabric 15 |
| Fabric 16 |
| Fabric 17 |
| Fabric 18 |
| Fabric 19 |
| Fabric 20 |

Make 2 of each.

ROW 1

Row 1 is the middle row of your quilt.

1. From a strip set with the seam allowances pressed up, cut three ¾"-wide slices. Refer to "Cutting Slices" on page 16 as needed for guidance.

2. Referring to your fabric map and using one slice, remove the stitching between fabrics 12 and 13 to make a segment with eight fabrics (fabrics 13–20). This becomes the top of row 1. Set aside the leftover segment for step 5.

3. On a second slice, remove the stitching between fabrics 2 and 3, so you have a segment with 18 fabrics (fabrics 3–20). With right sides together and using a scant ¼"-wide seam allowance, stitch fabric 3 to fabric 20 on the segment from step 2.

4. On the remaining slice, remove the stitching between fabrics 18 and 19 *and* between fabrics 6 and 7 to make a segment with 12 fabrics (fabrics 7–18). Stitch fabric 18 to fabric 20 on the bottom of the partial row from step 3. Fabric 7 will now be at the bottom of the row.

5. On the leftover segment from step 2, remove the stitching between fabrics 11 and 12. Using the segment with 11 fabrics, stitch fabric 1 to fabric 7 at the bottom of the row. You now have a complete row. Using your fabric map as a guide, compare your finished row to row 1 on the Aurora Borealis Design Chart on page 23. The numbers assigned to your fabrics should be in the same order as the chart numbers for row 1. You should have 49 fabrics in your row.

6. Check the pressing direction of the entire strip; make sure all the seam allowances are pressed toward the top of the row.

ROW 2

Make two identical rows.

1. Using a strip set that has the seam allowances pressed down, cut six 1"-wide slices.

2. Referring to your fabric map and using one slice, remove the stitching between fabrics 13 and 14. The segment with fabrics 14–20 becomes the top of row 2. Set aside the leftover segment for step 5.

3. Using a full slice (fabrics 1–20), stitch fabric 1 to fabric 20 on the segment from step 2.

4. On another slice, remove the stitching between fabrics 16 *and* 17 *and* between fabrics 6 and 7 to make a segment with 10 fabrics. Using the segment with fabrics 7–16, stitch fabric 16 to fabric 20 on the bottom of the partial row from step 3. Fabric 7 will now be at the bottom of the row.

5. On the leftover segment from step 2, remove the stitching between fabrics 12 and 13. Using the segment with 12 fabrics, stitch fabric 1 to fabric 7 at the bottom of the row. You now have a complete row. In the same manner, make a second identical row 2.

6. Compare the two rows to each other and to the chart for accuracy. Press all seam allowances in these two rows toward the bottom of the row.

7. Lay the rows on your ironing board side by side with row 1 in the middle. They should all be the same length and contain 49 pieces of fabric, in the number sequence indicated on the chart.

JOINING THE ROWS

Sew a row 2 to either side of row 1 before assembling row 3.

1. With right sides together and raw edges aligned, place row 2 on top of row 1. Using a scant ¼"-wide seam allowance, join the rows along their long edges, carefully matching the seam intersections with your finger. You may want to use a stylus or an awl to hold the matched seam intersections in place, gently easing the fabric as needed to align the seams.

2. Press the seam allowances toward the newly added rows—away from the quilt center—before sewing the second row 2. This center portion of the quilt is the hardest area to press because the finished center row is only ¼" wide. As the quilt top grows larger it becomes much easier to handle.

3. Place the second row 2 on top of row 1, right sides together and raw edges aligned. Join the rows along their long edges, carefully matching the seam intersections.

Alternate Stitching Direction

When joining subsequent pairs of rows (after row 2), you'll need to alternate the stitching direction from one side of the quilt to the other. On one side of the quilt, sew from the top of the row to the bottom. On the other side of the quilt, sew from the bottom of the row to the top. You'll find that sewing with the narrow single row on top and the larger quilt section on the bottom makes joining the rows easier and gives you more control when matching seam inter-sections. One direction may seem easier to sew, but if you continue in this manner throughout the project you'll get used to crossing seam allowances that feel like they are going the wrong direction.

WORKING FROM THE CHART

1. Continue working in this manner; for each pair of rows cut six slices in the width indicated on the chart. Referring to your fabric map and using the bold lines on the chart as a guide, remove the stitching between segments, as needed, and join the segments in the order indicated for the row you are making. Each time you'll be making two identical rows. Be sure to alternate your cutting between the strip sets so that the odd-number rows (3, 5, 7, etc.) have the seam allowances pressed up and the even-number rows (4, 6, 8, etc) have the seam allowances pressed down.

2. After completing each new pair of rows, check that they match the chart and that they are the same length as the center unit.

3. Join each new pair of rows to opposite sides of the quilt center, alternating the stitching direction and pressing the seam allowances toward the newly added rows, before working on the next pair of rows.

CREATING ADDITIONAL SECTIONS

Once you have completed and added row 9 to each side, begin making two new sections, each with rows 10–17. I find that dividing the project into three sections makes it easier to handle.

1. Continue working in the same manner as described before until you have worked all the way across the chart, adding identical rows to each section. Make sure you have a right side and mirror-image left side that can be joined to the center section to complete the symmetrical design.

2. Join your three sections in the correct numerical order to complete the center of your quilt top.

BORDERS AND FINISHING

1. Refer to "Borders with Mitered Corners" on page 89 to make a border unit using the 1½"-wide inner-border strips, 1"-wide border accent strips, and the 3½"-wide outer-border strips. Measure, cut, and sew the border unit to the quilt top.

2. Layer the quilt top with batting and backing. Baste and quilt, referring to pages 92 and 93 as needed. (Or take the neatly folded quilt top and backing to a professional long-arm machine quilter.)

3. If you want to hang your quilt, add a hanging sleeve as described on page 93. Using the 2¼"-wide binding strips and referring to "Binding" on page 94, make and attach the binding.

Quilt layout

Begin working with Row 1 (far right), which is the center of the quilt.
Make two of each subsequent row and place them on either side of the quilt center so that the design forms a mirror image.

Row number	17	16	15	14	13	12	11	10	9	8	7	6	5	4	3	2	1
Cut width of rows	1"	1¼"	1¼"	1½"	1½"	2"	2"	2¼"	2"	2"	1½"	1½"	1¼"	1¼"	1"	1"	¾"
Fabric number	9	8	7	6	5	4	3	2	1	20	19	18	17	16	15	14	13
	10	9	8	7	6	5	4	3	2	1	20	19	18	17	16	15	14
	11	10	9	8	7	6	5	4	3	2	1	20	19	18	17	16	15
	12	11	10	9	8	7	6	5	4	3	2	1	20	19	18	17	16
	13	12	11	10	9	8	7	6	5	4	3	2	1	20	19	18	17
	14	13	12	11	10	9	8	7	6	5	4	3	2	1	20	19	18
	15	14	13	12	11	10	9	8	7	6	5	4	3	2	1	20	19
	16	15	14	13	12	11	10	9	8	7	6	5	4	3	2	1	20
	17	16	15	14	13	12	11	10	9	8	7	6	5	4	1	2	3
	18	17	16	15	14	13	12	11	10	9	8	7	6	1	2	3	4
	19	18	17	16	15	14	13	12	11	10	9	8	1	2	3	4	5
	20	19	18	17	16	15	14	13	12	11	10	1	2	3	4	5	6
	16	20	19	18	17	16	15	14	13	12	1	2	3	4	5	6	7
	15	16	20	19	18	17	16	15	14	1	2	3	4	5	6	7	8
	14	15	16	20	19	18	17	16	1	2	3	4	5	6	7	8	9
	13	14	15	16	20	19	18	1	2	3	4	5	6	7	8	9	10
	12	13	14	15	16	20	1	2	3	4	5	6	7	8	9	10	11
	11	12	13	14	15	1	2	3	4	5	6	7	8	9	10	11	12
	10	11	12	13	1	2	3	4	5	6	7	8	9	10	11	12	13
	9	10	11	1	2	3	4	5	6	7	8	9	10	11	12	13	14
	8	9	1	2	3	4	5	6	7	8	9	10	11	12	13	14	15
	7	1	2	3	4	5	6	7	8	9	10	11	12	13	14	15	16
	1	2	3	4	5	6	7	8	9	10	11	12	13	14	15	16	17
	2	1	4	5	6	7	8	9	10	11	12	13	14	15	16	17	18
	3	2	1	6	7	8	9	10	11	12	13	14	15	16	17	18	19
	4	3	2	1	8	9	10	11	12	13	14	15	16	17	18	19	20
	5	4	3	2	1	10	11	12	13	14	15	16	17	18	19	20	18
	6	5	4	3	2	1	12	13	14	15	16	17	18	19	20	16	17
	7	6	5	4	3	2	1	14	15	16	17	18	19	20	14	15	16
	8	7	6	5	4	3	2	1	16	17	18	19	20	12	13	14	15
	9	8	7	6	5	4	3	2	1	18	19	20	10	11	12	13	14
	10	9	8	7	6	5	4	3	2	1	20	8	9	10	11	12	13
	11	10	9	8	7	6	5	4	3	2	1	7	8	9	10	11	12
	12	11	10	9	8	7	6	5	4	3	2	1	7	8	9	10	11
	13	12	11	10	9	8	7	6	5	4	3	2	1	7	8	9	10
	14	13	12	11	10	9	8	7	6	5	4	3	2	1	7	8	9
	15	14	13	12	11	10	9	8	7	6	5	4	3	2	1	7	8
	16	15	14	13	12	11	10	9	8	7	6	5	4	3	2	1	7
	17	16	15	14	13	12	11	10	9	8	7	6	5	4	3	2	1
	18	17	16	15	14	13	12	11	10	9	8	7	6	5	4	3	2
	19	18	17	16	15	14	13	12	11	10	9	8	7	6	5	4	3
	20	19	18	17	16	15	14	13	12	11	10	9	8	7	6	5	4
	19	20	19	18	17	16	15	14	13	12	11	10	9	8	7	6	5
	18	19	20	19	18	17	16	15	14	13	12	11	10	9	8	7	6
	17	18	19	20	19	18	17	16	15	14	13	12	11	10	9	8	7
	16	17	18	19	20	19	18	17	16	15	14	13	12	11	10	9	8
	15	16	17	18	19	20	19	18	17	16	15	14	13	12	11	10	9
	14	15	16	17	18	19	20	19	18	17	16	15	14	13	12	11	10
	13	14	15	16	17	18	19	20	19	18	17	16	15	14	13	12	11

ISLAND SUNSET

"Island Sunset" was my second attempt at twisting a bargello into an unusual shape. It's based on a prototype that had evolved when I was working on "Aurora Borealis" (page 18). The colors were reminiscent of a strange but beautiful sunset picture I had taken very late on a summer night when it was actually quite dark, but the sky was strangely lit with browns, oranges, and reds, just before the sun disappeared. I had never worked in these colors before, but a beautiful night sky seemed like a suitable palette for a change of pace.

CHOOSING FABRIC

This quilt uses 20 fabrics in two color groups: 12 in lighter or brighter colors and 8 in a darker color group. Fabrics in each color group should range from light to dark. I recommend you wait until the bargello center is finished to choose fabric for the border because fabrics can take on a new life when they are sewn together. I suggest a dark fabric that enhances the overall appearance of your project and frames it nicely, plus a bright border accent. The border should enhance the total appearance of the quilt as well as frame it.

MATERIALS

Yardage is based on 42"-wide fabric.

¼ yard *each* of 12 lighter/brighter bargello fabrics

¼ yard *each* of 8 darker bargello fabrics

1⅜ yards of a dark fabric for borders and binding

¼ yard of a bright fabric for border accent

3⅛ yards of fabric for backing

48" x 65" piece of batting

CUTTING

From *each* of the 20 bargello fabrics, cut:
4 strips, 1½" x 42"

From the dark fabric for borders and binding, cut:
6 outer-border strips, 3½" x 42"
6 binding strips, 2¼" x 42"
6 inner-border strips, 1½" x 42"

From the bright fabric for border accent, cut:
6 strips, 1" x 42"

Finished Size: 40¼" x 56½"   ▪   Pieced and machine quilted by author

FABRIC MAP

Referring to page 13, use a scrap of each of your bargello fabrics to create a fabric map. You'll need to refer to your map throughout the project in order to position all of your strips correctly to make the design shown. For the quilt on page 25, fabric 1 is yellow and fabric 20 is the darkest brown.

MAKING THE STRIP SETS

Referring to "Building Strip Sets" on page 14 and using the 1½"-wide bargello fabric strips, sew the strips together in numerical order according to your fabric map to make four identical strip sets. On two strip sets, press the seam allowances *up*, toward fabric

On the remaining two strip sets, press the seam allowances *down*, toward fabric 20. Cut all odd-number rows from the strip sets with the seam allowances pressed up and all even-number rows from the strip sets with the seam allowances pressed down.

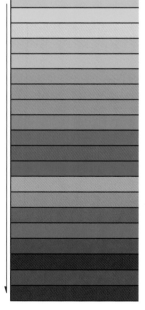

Make 2 of each.

ROW 1

Row 1 is the middle row of your quilt.

1. From a strip set with the seam allowances pressed up, cut three ¾"-wide slices. Refer to "Cutting Slices" on page 16 as needed for guidance.

2. Referring to your fabric map and using one slice, remove the stitching between fabrics 14 and 15 to make a segment with six fabrics (fabrics 15–20). This becomes the top of row 1. Set aside the leftover segment for step 5.

3. Using a full slice (fabrics 1–20), stitch fabric 1 to fabric 20 on the segment from step 2, right sides together and using a scant ¼"-wide seam allowance.

4. On the remaining slice, remove the stitching between fabrics 16 and 17 *and* between fabrics 6 and 7 to make a segment with 10 fabrics (fabrics 7–16). Stitch fabric 16 to fabric 20 on the bottom of the partial row from step 3. Fabric 7 will now be at the bottom of the row. Set aside the leftover segment for step 6.

5. On the leftover segment from step 2, remove the stitching between fabrics 8 and 9. Using the segment with eight fabrics, stitch fabric 1 to fabric 7 on the bottom of the partial row from step 4. Fabric 8 will now be at the bottom of the row.

6. On the leftover segment from step 4, remove the stitching between fabrics 4 and 5. Using the segment with four fabrics, stitch fabric 1 to fabric 8 on the bottom of the row. You now have a complete row. Using your fabric map as a guide, compare your finished row to row 1 on the Island Sunset Design Chart on page 29. The numbers assigned to your fabrics should be in the same order as the chart numbers for row 1. You should have 48 fabrics in your row.

7. Check the pressing direction of the entire strip; make sure all the seam allowances are pressed toward the top of the row.

ROW 2

Make two identical rows.

1. Using a strip set that has the seam allowances pressed down, cut six 1"-wide slices.

2. Referring to your fabric map and using one slice, remove the stitching between fabrics 15 and 16. The segment with fabrics 16–20 becomes the top of row 2. Set aside the leftover segment for step 7.

3. Using a full slice (fabrics 1–20), stitch fabric 1 to fabric 20 on the segment from step 2.

4. On another slice, remove the stitching between fabrics 18 and 19 to make a two-fabric segment. Stitch fabric 19 to fabric 20 on the bottom of the partial row from step 3.

5. On the remaining segment from step 4, remove the stitching between fabrics 16 and 17 *and* between fabrics 6 and 7. Using the segment with fabrics 7–16, stitch fabric 16 to fabric 20 on the bottom of the partial row from step 4. Fabric 7 will now be at the bottom of the row.

6. Using the segment with six fabrics (fabrics 1–6) from step 5, stitch fabric 1 to fabric 7 at the bottom of the row.

7. On the leftover segment from step 2, remove the stitching between fabrics 5 and 6. Stitch fabric 1 to fabric 6 on the bottom of the row. You now have a complete row. In the same manner, make a second identical row 2.

8. Compare the two rows to each other and to the chart for accuracy. Press all seam allowances in these two rows toward the bottom of the row.

9. Lay the rows on your ironing board side by side with row 1 in the middle. They should all be the same length and contain 48 pieces of fabric, in the number sequence indicated on the chart.

JOINING THE ROWS

Sew a row 2 to either side of row 1 before assembling row 3.

1. With right sides together and raw edges aligned, place row 2 on top of row 1. Using a scant $\frac{1}{4}$"-wide seam allowance, join the rows along their long edges, carefully matching the seam intersections with your finger. You may want to use a stylus or an awl to hold the matched seam intersections in place, gently easing the fabric as needed to align the seams.

2. Press the seam allowances toward the newly added rows—away from the quilt center—before sewing the second row 2. This center portion of the quilt is the hardest area to press because the center row is only $\frac{1}{4}$" wide when finished. As the quilt top grows larger it becomes much easier to handle.

3. Place the second row 2 on top of row 1, right sides together and raw edges aligned. Join the rows along their long edges, carefully matching the seam intersections. See the "Alternate Stitching Direction" box on page 21.

WORKING FROM THE CHART

1. Continue working in this manner; for each pair of rows cut six slices in the width indicated on the chart. Referring to your fabric map and using the bold lines on the chart as a guide, remove the stitching between segments, as needed, and sew the segments together in the order indicated for the row you are making. Each time you'll be making two identical rows. Be sure to alternate your cutting between the strip sets so that the odd-number rows (3, 5, 7, etc.) have the seam allowances pressed up and the even-number rows (4, 6, 8, etc.) have the seam allowances pressed down.

2. After completing each new pair of rows, check that they match the chart and that they are the same length as the center unit.

3. Join each new pair of rows to opposite sides of the quilt center, alternating the stitching direction and pressing the seam allowances toward the newly added rows, before working on the next pair of rows.

CREATING ADDITIONAL SECTIONS

Once you have completed and added row 10 to each side, you might want to begin two new sections, each with rows 11–20. I find that dividing the project into three sections makes it easier to handle.

1. Continue working in the same manner as described above until you have worked all the way across the chart, adding identical rows to each side of the center. Make sure you have a right side and mirror-image left side that can be joined to the center section to complete the symmetrical design.

2. To complete rows 18–20, use leftover segments for the bottom pieces beginning with fabric 19 in row 18.

3. Join the three sections in the correct numerical order to complete the center of your quilt top.

BORDERS AND FINISHING

1. Refer to "Borders with Mitered Corners" on page 89 to make a border unit using the 1½"-wide inner-border strips, 1"-wide border accent strips, and the 3½"-wide outer-border strips. Measure, cut, and sew the border unit to the quilt top.

2. Layer the quilt top with batting and backing. Baste and quilt, referring to pages 92 and 93 as needed. (Or take the neatly folded quilt top and backing to a professional long-arm machine quilter.)

3. If you want to hang your quilt, add a hanging sleeve as described on page 93. Using the 2¼"-wide binding strips and referring to "Binding" on page 94, make and attach the binding.

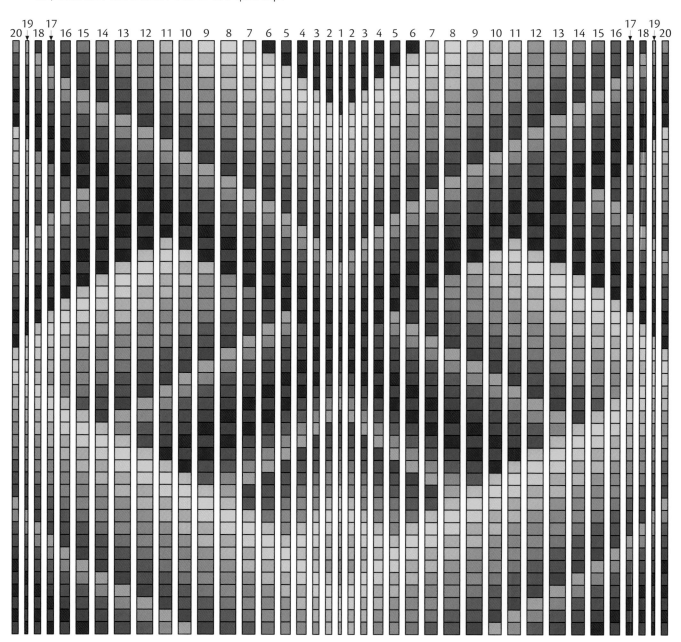

Quilt layout

ISLAND SUNSET DESIGN CHART

Begin working with Row 1 (far right), which is the center of the quilt. Make two of each subsequent row and place them on either side of the quilt center so that the design forms a mirror image.

Row number	20	19	18	17	16	15	14	13	12	11	10	9	8	7	6	5	4	3	2	1
Cut width of rows	1"	¾"	1"	1"	1¼"	1½"	1½"	1¾"	1¾"	1½"	1½"	1¾"	1¾"	1½"	1½"	1¼"	1¼"	1"	1"	¾"
Fabric number	14	13	12	11	10	9	8	7	6	5	4	3	2	1	20	19	18	17	16	15
	15	14	13	12	11	10	9	8	7	6	5	4	3	2	1	20	19	18	17	16
	16	15	14	13	12	11	10	9	8	7	6	5	4	3	2	1	20	19	18	17
	17	16	15	14	13	12	11	10	9	8	7	6	5	4	3	2	1	20	19	18
	18	17	16	15	14	13	12	11	10	9	8	7	6	5	4	3	2	1	20	19
	19	18	17	16	15	14	13	12	11	10	9	8	7	6	5	4	3	2	1	20
	20	19	18	17	16	15	14	13	12	11	10	9	8	7	6	5	4	3	2	1
	3	20	19	18	17	16	15	14	13	12	11	10	9	8	7	6	5	4	3	2
	4	5	20	19	18	17	16	15	14	13	12	11	10	9	8	7	6	5	4	3
	5	6	7	20	19	18	17	16	15	14	13	12	11	10	9	8	7	6	5	4
	6	7	8	9	20	19	18	17	16	15	14	13	12	11	10	9	8	7	6	5
	7	8	9	10	11	20	19	18	17	16	15	14	13	12	11	10	9	8	7	6
	8	9	10	11	12	13	20	19	18	17	16	15	14	13	12	11	10	9	8	7
	9	10	11	12	13	14	15	20	19	18	17	16	15	14	13	12	11	10	9	8
	10	11	12	13	14	15	16	17	20	19	18	17	16	15	14	13	12	11	10	9
	11	12	13	14	15	16	17	18	19	20	19	18	17	16	15	14	13	12	11	10
	12	13	14	15	16	17	18	19	20	1	20	19	18	17	16	15	14	13	12	11
	13	14	15	16	17	18	19	20	1	2	3	20	19	18	17	16	15	14	13	12
	14	15	16	17	18	19	20	1	2	3	4	5	20	19	18	17	16	15	14	13
	15	16	17	18	19	20	1	2	3	4	5	6	7	20	19	18	17	16	15	14
	16	17	18	19	20	1	2	3	4	5	6	7	8	9	20	19	18	17	16	15
	17	18	19	20	1	2	3	4	5	6	7	8	9	10	11	20	19	18	17	16
	18	19	20	1	2	3	4	5	6	7	8	9	10	11	12	13	20	19	18	17
	19	20	1	2	3	4	5	6	7	8	9	10	11	12	13	14	15	20	19	18
	20	1	2	3	4	5	6	7	8	9	10	11	12	13	14	15	16	17	20	19
	1	2	3	4	5	6	7	8	9	10	11	12	13	14	15	16	17	18	19	20
	2	1	4	5	6	7	8	9	10	11	12	13	14	15	16	17	18	19	20	16
	3	2	1	6	7	8	9	10	11	12	13	14	15	16	17	18	19	20	16	15
	4	3	2	1	8	9	10	11	12	13	14	15	16	17	18	19	20	16	15	14
	5	4	3	2	1	10	11	12	13	14	15	16	17	18	19	20	16	15	14	13
	6	5	4	3	2	1	12	13	14	15	16	17	18	19	20	16	15	14	13	12
	7	6	5	4	3	2	1	14	15	16	17	18	19	20	16	15	14	13	12	11
	8	7	6	5	4	3	2	1	16	17	18	19	20	16	15	14	13	12	11	10
	9	8	7	6	5	4	3	2	1	18	19	20	16	15	14	13	12	11	10	9
	10	9	8	7	6	5	4	3	2	1	20	16	15	14	13	12	11	10	9	8
	11	10	9	8	7	6	5	4	3	2	1	15	14	13	12	11	10	9	8	7
	12	11	10	9	8	7	6	5	4	3	2	1	13	12	11	10	9	8	7	1
	13	12	11	10	9	8	7	6	5	4	3	2	1	11	10	9	8	7	1	2
	14	13	12	11	10	9	8	7	6	5	4	3	2	1	9	8	7	1	2	3
	15	14	13	12	11	10	9	8	7	6	5	4	3	2	1	7	1	2	3	4
	16	15	14	13	12	11	10	9	8	7	6	5	4	3	2	1	2	3	4	5
	17	16	15	14	13	12	11	10	9	8	7	6	5	4	3	2	1	4	5	6
	18	17	16	15	14	13	12	11	10	9	8	7	6	5	4	3	2	1	6	7
	19	18	17	16	15	14	13	12	11	10	9	8	7	6	5	4	3	2	1	8
	20	19	18	17	16	15	14	13	12	11	10	9	8	7	6	5	4	3	2	1
	19	20	19	18	17	16	15	14	13	12	11	10	9	8	7	6	5	4	3	2
	18	19	20	19	18	17	16	15	14	13	12	11	10	9	8	7	6	5	4	3
	17	18	19	20	19	18	17	16	15	14	13	12	11	10	9	8	7	6	5	4

COSMIC TWIST

"Cosmic Twist" was my first computer-designed twisted bargello quilt. Although the program I used was designed for creating "normal" bargello, I was able to change the numbers out of sequence to create the kind of quilt I wanted to make. It isn't symmetrical, although it almost looks like it is, so it's constructed slightly differently than "Aurora Borealis" on page 18.

CHOOSING FABRIC

This quilt uses 20 fabrics in two color groups: 5 in one color group (green) and 15 in a coordinating color group (blue). Fabrics in both color groups should range in value from light to dark and include one or two fabrics that consist of both colors. Think about adding one or two zinger fabrics to the mix.

MATERIALS

Yardage is based on 42"-wide fabric.

⅝ yard *each* of 20 fabrics for bargello

⅝ yard of a dark fabric for binding

5½ yards of fabric for backing

67" x 89" piece of batting

FABRIC MAP

Referring to page 13, use a scrap of each of your bargello fabrics to create a fabric map. You'll need to refer to this map throughout the project in order to position all of your strips correctly to make the design. For the quilt on page 31, fabric 1 is lime green and fabric 20 is the darkest blue.

Finished Size: 58¾" x 80½"

Pieced by author and machine quilted by Nadia Wilson of Port Hardy, British Columbia, Canada

CUTTING

From bargello fabrics 1–7 and 15–20, cut:
5 strips, 2½" x 42"

From *each* of the remaining 7 bargello fabrics: cut:
4 strips, 2½"x 42"

From the dark fabric for binding, cut:
8 strips, 2¼" x 42"

MAKING THE STRIP SETS

1. Referring to "Building Strip Sets" on page 14 and using the 2½"-wide bargello fabric strips, sew the strips together in numerical order according to your fabric map to make four identical strip sets. On two strip sets, press the seam allowances *up*, toward fabric 1. On the remaining two strip sets, press the seam allowances *down*, toward fabric 20. Cut all odd-number rows from the strip sets with the seam allowances pressed up and all even-number rows from the strip sets with the seam allowances pressed down.

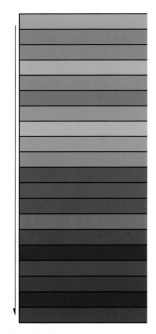

Fabric 1	
Fabric 2	
Fabric 3	
Fabric 4	
Fabric 5	
Fabric 6	
Fabric 7	
Fabric 8	
Fabric 9	
Fabric 10	
Fabric 11	
Fabric 12	
Fabric 13	
Fabric 14	
Fabric 15	
Fabric 16	
Fabric 17	
Fabric 18	
Fabric 19	
Fabric 20	

Make 2 of each.

2. Using the remaining bargello fabric strips, make one partial strip set using fabrics 1–7 and one partial strip set using fabrics 15–20. Press the seam allowances to one side for now. Later, you may need to change the pressing direction to match the other seam allowances in the row you're constructing.

Creating an Asymmetrical Quilt

"Cosmic Twist" isn't a symmetrical quilt so it's assembled starting on the far left with row 1 and working to row 39 on the far right. Unlike a symmetrical quilt, where you need to make an identical pair of each row (except for row 1), here, you'll only make one of each row. If you have a large design wall, I recommend making a few rows and pinning them to your design wall as you go. Then sew them together, pressing the seam allowances after adding each row. That way you'll have a preview of your quilt long before you reach row 39!

ROW 1

1. From a strip set with the seam allowances pressed up, cut two 1½"-wide slices. From a partial strip set with fabrics 1–7, cut one 1½"-wide slice. Refer to "Cutting Slices" on page 16 as needed for guidance.

2. Referring to your fabric map and using one full slice, remove the stitching between fabrics 18 and 19 to make a segment with fabrics 1–18. This becomes the top of row 1.

3. Using a full slice (fabrics 1–20), stitch fabric 1 to fabric 18 on the segment from step 2, right sides together and using a scant ¼"-wide seam allowance.

4. On the slice from the partial strip set, remove the stitching between fabrics 2 and 3 to make a two-fabric segment. Stitch fabric 1 to fabric 20 on the bottom of the row. You now have a complete row. Using your fabric map as a guide, compare your finished row to row 1 on the Cosmic Twist Design Chart on page 35. The numbers assigned to your fabrics should be in the same order as the chart numbers for row 1. You should have 40 fabrics in your row.

5. Check the pressing direction of the entire strip; make sure all the seam allowances are pressed toward the top of the row.

ROW 2

1. From a strip set with the seam allowances pressed down, cut two 1½"-wide slices. From a partial strip set with fabrics 1–7, cut one 1½"-wide slice.

2. Referring to your fabric map and using one full slice, remove the stitching between fabrics 19 and 20 *and* between fabrics 16 and 17 to make a single piece of fabric 20 and a segment with fabrics 1–16. Stitch fabric 1 to the fabric 20 piece. Fabric 16 will now be at the bottom of the row.

3. Using a full slice, stitch fabric 1 to fabric 16 at the bottom of the partial row from step 2.

4. On the slice from the partial strip set, remove the stitching between fabrics 3 and 4 to make a three-fabric segment. Stitch fabric 1 to fabric 20 on the bottom of the row. You now have a complete row. Using your fabric map as a guide, compare your finished row to row 2 on the chart. The numbers assigned to your fabrics should be in the same order as the chart numbers for row 2.

5. Check the pressing direction of the entire strip; make sure all the seam allowances are pressed toward the bottom of the row. Lay row 1 and row 2 on your ironing board; the rows should be the same length.

JOINING THE ROWS

With right sides together and raw edges aligned, place row 2 on top of row 1. Using a scant ¼"-wide seam allowance and carefully matching the seam intersections with your finger, join the rows along their long edges, sewing from the top of the row to the bottom. You may want to use a stylus or an awl to hold the matched seam intersections in place, gently easing the fabric as needed to align the seams. Press the seam allowances toward the newly added rows, in this case, row 2.

ROW 3

1. From a strip set with the seam allowances pressed up, cut two 1¾"-wide slices. From the partial strip set with fabrics 1–7, cut one 1¾"-wide slice.

2. Using one full slice, remove the stitching between fabrics 18 and 19 *and* between fabrics 14 and 15 to make a two-piece segment and a segment with fabrics 1–14. Stitch fabric 1 to fabric 20 on the two-fabric segment. Fabric 14 will be at the bottom of the row.

3. Using a full slice, stitch fabric 1 to fabric 14 on the bottom of the partial row from step 2.

4. On the slice from the partial strip set, remove the stitching between fabrics 4 and 5 to make a four-fabric segment. Stitch fabric 1 to fabric 20 at the bottom of the row. You now have a complete row. Compare your finished row to row 3 on the chart. The numbers assigned to your fabrics should match the chart numbers for row 3.

5. Check the pressing direction of the entire strip; make sure all the seam allowances are pressed toward the top of the row. Compare the length of row 3 to the sewn section with rows 1 and 2; the rows should all be the same length.

6. Stitch row 3 to row 2 in the same manner as before, pressing the seam allowances toward the newly added row.

WORKING FROM THE CHART

1. Continue working in this manner; for each row cut two full slices in the width indicated on the chart. Referring to your fabric map and using the bold lines on the chart as a guide, remove the stitching between segments, as needed, and join the segments in the order indicated for the row you are making. Make one row at a time, working across the chart. Be sure to alternate your cutting between the strip sets so that the odd-number rows (3, 5, 7, etc.) have the seam allowances pressed up and the even-number rows (4, 6, 8, etc) have the seam allowances pressed down.

2. From the partial strip set with fabrics 1–7, cut one slice in the width indicated on the chart for rows 4–9 and rows 20–28. From the partial strip set with fabrics 15–20, cut one slice in the width indicated on the chart for rows 10–18 and rows 31–38. (Rows 19, 29, 30, and 39 do not require slices cut from the partial strip sets.)

3. You can join the rows as you make each new row, or you can pin rows to your design wall and then sew the rows together after several rows are completed, whichever method works best for you.

4. Once all the rows are sewn together, finish by basting around the quilt top about 1/8" from the outer edges to stabilize the seams for quilting.

FINISHING

1. Layer the quilt top with batting and backing. Baste and quilt, referring to pages 92 and 93 as needed. (Or take the neatly folded quilt top and backing to a professional long-arm machine quilter.)

2. If you want to hang your quilt, add a hanging sleeve as described on page 93. Using the 2¼"-wide binding strips and referring to "Binding" on page 94, make and attach the binding.

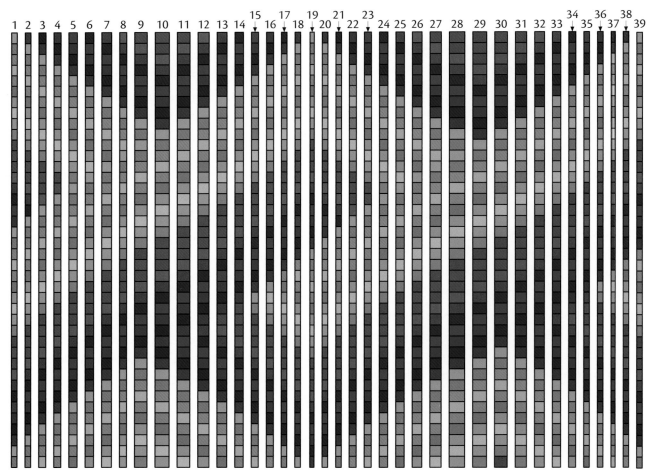

Quilt layout

Row number	Cut width of row	Fabric number
1	1½"	
2	1½"	
3	1¾"	
4	1¾"	
5	2"	
6	2"	
7	2¼"	
8	2½"	
9	2¾"	
10	3"	
11	2¾"	
12	2½"	
13	2¼"	
14	2"	
15	1¾"	
16	1¾"	
17	1½"	
18	1½"	
19	1¼"	
20	1½"	
21	1½"	
22	1¾"	
23	1¾"	
24	2"	
25	2"	
26	2¼"	
27	2½"	
28	2¾"	
29	3"	
30	2¾"	
31	2½"	
32	2¼"	
33	2"	
34	1¾"	
35	1½"	
36	1½"	
37	1¼"	
38	1½"	
39	1½"	

SUPERNOVA

When I decided to design a bed-sized quilt, I spent a lot of time playing in my funny little bargello computer program, and "Supernova" is what I finally came up with. I love how the colors glow. One friend called it a molten embrace. This quilt size works well as a bedspread on a double bed but will also fit a queen-size bed. You only need to add a border to make it king size. To make the construction of this quilt top easier, I made two separate halves and then joined the halves together. To see a gorgeous blue-and-purple version that a friend made, turn to page 86.

CHOOSING FABRICS

Select 20 fabrics in one color group; the colors should range in value from light to dark.

MATERIALS

Yardage is based on 42"-wide fabric.

⅞ yard each of 20 bargello fabrics

⅞ yard of a dark fabric for binding

9¼ yards of fabric for backing

105" x 107" piece of batting

CUTTING

From each of the 20 bargello fabrics, cut:
8 or 9 strips, 2½" x 42"

From the dark fabric for binding, cut:
11 strips, 2¼" x 42"

Start with a Few...

You will need at least 8 strip sets to build the quilt and possibly 9 or 10 depending on the width of your narrowest fabric and how frequently you make use of leftover partial segments. Since you still need slices with seam allowances pressed in alternating directions, you may wish to create eight full-width strip sets and then make two half-width strip sets if you find you require a few more segments.

Finished Size: 96½" x 98½"

Pieced by author and machine quilted by Pat and Don Bays of Nanaimo, British Columbia, Canada

FABRIC MAP

Referring to page 13, use a scrap of each of your bargello fabrics to create a fabric map showing your fabrics in light to dark order with their assigned numbers from 1–20 (fabric 1 is the lightest fabric and fabric 20 is the darkest one). You'll need this through-out the entire project in order to position all of your strips correctly to make the design as shown.

MAKING THE STRIP SETS

Referring to "Building Strip Sets" on page 14 and using the 2½"-wide bargello fabric strips, sew the strips together in numerical order according to your fabric map to make eight identical strip sets. On four strip sets, press the seam allowances *up*, toward fabric

On the remaining four strip sets, press the seam allowances *down*, toward fabric 20. Cut all odd-number rows from the strip sets with the seam allowances pressed up and all even-number rows from the strip sets with the seam allowances pressed down.

Make 4 of each.

Additional Strip Sets

Wait to make any additional strip sets until you start building the bottom half of the quilt and see how many leftover segments you can utilize from the top half. You might find that a strip set of fabrics 1–8 is all you need to finish the bottom half.

ASSEMBLING THE TOP HALF

This quilt is built in two halves. The top half consists of 25 fabrics in each row and the bottom half has 24 fabrics per row. Both halves are constructed separately and then joined together to complete the quilt top.

Row 1

Row 1 is the middle row of your quilt.

1. From a strip set with the seam allowances pressed up, cut two 1½"-wide slices. Refer to "Cutting Slices" on page 16 as needed for guidance.

2. Referring to your fabric map and using one slice, remove the stitching between fabrics 19 and 20 *and* between fabrics 15 and 16 to make a segment with fabrics 16–19. Set aside the leftover segment for step 4.

3. Use a full slice (fabrics 1–20) and stitch fabric 20 to fabric 19 on the segment from step 2. Fabric 1 becomes the top of row 1.

4. On the leftover segment from step 2, remove the stitching between fabrics 1 and 2 and stitch the single piece of fabric 1 to fabric 16 at the bottom of your row. You now have a complete row. Using your fabric map as a guide, compare your finished row to row 1 on the Supernova Design Chart (top half) on page 42. The numbers assigned to your fabrics should be in the same order as the chart numbers for row 1. You should have 25 fabrics in your row.

5. Check the pressing direction of the entire strip; make sure all the seam allowances are pressed toward the top of the row. Set aside any leftover segments for possible use later.

Row 2

Make two identical rows.

1. From a strip set that has the seam allowances pressed down, cut four 1¾"-wide slices.

2. Referring to your fabric map and using one slice, remove the stitching between fabrics 19 and 20. Stitch the single piece of fabric 20 to fabric 1 on the same slice. Fabric 20 becomes the top of row 2.

3. On another slice, remove the stitching between fabrics 17 and 18 and between fabrics 2 and 3. Use the segment with fabrics 18–20 and stitch fabric 20 to fabric 19 on the bottom of the partial row from step 2. Fabric 18 will now be at the bottom of the row.

4. Using the two-fabric segment from step 3, stitch fabric 1 to fabric 18 at the bottom of the row. You now have a complete row. In the same manner, make a second identical row 2. Set aside any leftover segments for possible use later.

5. Compare the two rows to each other and to the chart for accuracy. Press all seam allowances in these two rows toward the bottom of the row.

6. Lay the rows on your ironing board side by side with row 1 in the middle. They should all be the same length and in the number sequence indicated on the chart.

Organize Leftover Segments

You may find it helpful to organize your leftover segments by pinning them to your design wall, grouping segments from slices of equal width together.

Joining the Rows

Sew a row 2 to either side of row 1 before assembling row 3.

1. With right sides together and raw edges aligned, place row 2 on top of row 1. Using a scant ¼"-wide seam allowance, join the rows along their long edges, carefully matching the seam intersections with your finger. You may want to use a stylus or an awl to hold the matched seam intersections in place, gently easing the fabric as needed to align the seams. Press the seam allowances toward the newly added rows—away from the quilt center—before sewing the second row 2.

2. Place the second row 2 on top of row 1, right sides together and raw edges aligned. Join the rows along their long edges, carefully matching the seam intersections. See the "Alternate Stitching Direction" box on page 21.

Keeping Track

For easy reference, use a couple of sticky notes on the chart to cover up the rows you've completed and clearly mark the row you are currently building.

WORKING FROM THE CHART

1. Continue working in this manner; for each pair of rows, through row 12, cut four slices in the width indicated on the chart. Referring to your fabric map and using the bold lines on the chart as a guide, remove the stitching between segments, as needed, and join the segments in the order indicated on the chart for the row you are making. You'll be making two identical rows each time. Be sure to alternate your cutting between the strip sets so that the odd-number rows (3, 5, 7, etc.) have the seam allowances pressed up and the even-number rows (4, 6, 8, etc) have the seam allowances pressed down.

2. For each pair of rows 13–25, start by cutting two slices in the width indicated on the chart. At this point, you may be able to use some of the leftover segments to complete the rows. In the same manner as before, refer to your fabric map and join segments in the order indicated on the chart.

3. After completing each new pair of rows, check that they match the chart and that they are the same length as the center section.

4. Join each new pair of rows to opposite sides of the center section, alternating the stitching direction and pressing the seam allowances toward the newly added rows before working on the next pair of rows.

CREATING ADDITIONAL SECTIONS

Once you have completed and added row 12 to each side, you might want to begin two new sections each with rows 13–25. I find that dividing the project into three sections makes it easier to handle.

1. Continue working in the same manner as described before until you have worked all the way across the chart, adding identical rows to each side of the center. Make sure you have a right side and mirror-image left side that can be joined to the center section.

2. Join the three sections in the correct numerical order to complete the symmetrical design for the top half of the quilt.

BOTTOM HALF

Once the bottom half of the quilt with 24 fabrics per row is completed and turned upside down, then the two halves can be joined together to complete the symmetrical design.

When the rows are joined, the seam allowances in the bottom half must be pressed toward the middle row so that they are pressed in the opposite direction from the top half, making it easier to sew the two halves together. Therefore, it's necessary to build the bottom half in two sections starting with row 25.

1. In the same manner as the top half, cut slices from the appropriate strip sets in the width indicated on the chart. Referring to your fabric map and the chart for the bottom half of the quilt, starting with row 25, remove the stitching between segments, as needed, and use any available leftover segments to build the rows. Join the segments in the order indicated on the chart for the row you are making. Each time you'll be making two identical rows.

2. After completing each new pair of rows, check that they match the chart and that they are the same length. Check the pressing direction of the entire row; make sure all the seam allowances are pressed in the same direction.

3. Refer to "Joining the Rows" and sew row 24 to row 25, pressing the seam allowances toward row 24. Continue working in the same manner as you did for the top half until you have worked all the way across the chart, making sure you have a right side and mirror-image left side that can be joined in the middle with row 1. You may wish to build the bottom half in four sections to make it easier to handle.

4. Make one of row 1. Join the sections in the correct numerical order with row 1 in the center, to complete the symmetrical design for the bottom half of the quilt. Turn the bottom half upside down so that it's a mirror image of the top half.

ASSEMBLY

1. Check to ensure that the bottom half mirrors the top half, referring to the chart as needed. Carefully pin the two halves together, matching the seam intersections.

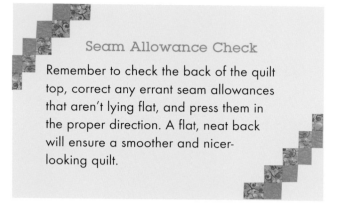

Seam Allowance Check

Remember to check the back of the quilt top, correct any errant seam allowances that aren't lying flat, and press them in the proper direction. A flat, neat back will ensure a smoother and nicer-looking quilt.

2. Use a scant ¼"-wide seam allowance to stitch the two halves together. Press the seam allowances to one side.

3. Finish by basting around the quilt top about ⅛" from the outer edges to stabilize the seams for quilting.

Make It King Size

If you want a king-size quilt, simply add a 5"- or 6"-wide border and your quilt will be 10" to 12" larger. A king-size quilt will require 12 or 13 binding strips.

FINISHING

1. Layer the quilt top with batting and backing. Baste and quilt, referring to pages 92 and 93 as needed. (Or take the neatly folded quilt top and backing to a professional long-arm machine quilter.)

2. If you want to hang your quilt, add a hanging sleeve as described on page 93. Using the 2¼"-wide binding strips and referring to "Binding" on page 94, make and attach the binding.

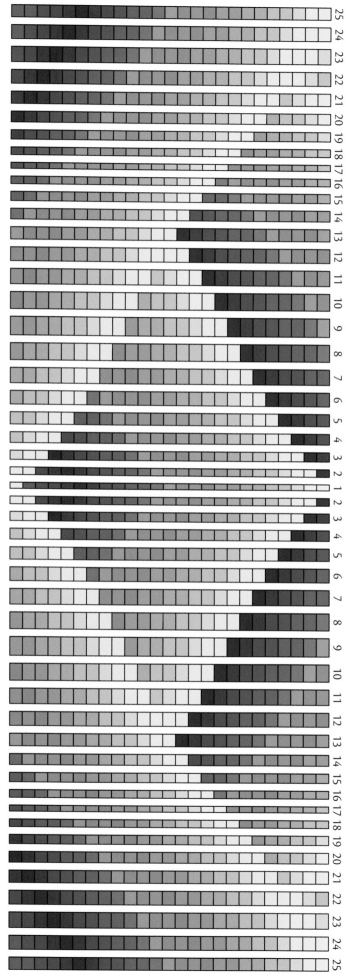

Quilt layout (top half)

SUPERNOVA DESIGN CHART

Top half of the quilt. Begin working with Row 1 (far right), which is the center of the quilt.
Make two of each subsequent row and place them on either side of the quilt center so that the design forms a mirror image.

Row number	25	24	23	22	21	20	19	18	17	16	15	14	13	12	11	10	9	8	7	6	5	4	3	2	1
Cut width of rows	2½"	2¾"	3"	2¾"	2½"	2¼"	2"	1¾"	1½"	1¾"	2"	2¼"	2½"	2¾"	3"	3¼"	3½"	3¼"	3"	2¾"	2½"	2¼"	2"	1¾"	1½"
Fabric number	1	2	3	4	1	2	3	4	5	6	7	8	9	10	11	12	13	14	15	16	17	18	19	20	1
	2	1	2	3	2	3	4	5	6	7	8	9	10	11	12	13	14	15	16	17	18	19	20	1	2
	3	2	1	2	3	4	5	6	7	8	9	10	11	12	13	14	15	16	17	18	19	20	1	2	3
	4	3	2	1	4	5	6	7	8	9	10	11	12	13	14	15	16	17	18	19	20	1	2	3	4
	5	4	3	2	1	6	7	8	9	10	11	12	13	14	15	16	17	18	19	20	1	2	3	4	5
	6	5	4	3	2	1	8	9	10	11	12	13	14	15	16	17	18	19	20	1	2	3	4	5	6
	7	6	5	4	3	2	1	10	11	12	13	14	15	16	17	18	19	20	1	2	3	4	5	6	7
	8	7	6	5	4	3	2	1	12	13	14	15	16	17	18	19	20	1	2	3	4	5	6	7	8
	9	8	7	6	5	4	3	2	1	14	15	16	17	18	19	20	1	2	3	4	5	6	7	8	9
	10	9	8	7	6	5	4	3	2	1	16	17	18	19	20	1	2	3	4	5	6	7	8	9	10
	11	10	9	8	7	6	5	4	3	2	1	18	19	20	1	2	3	4	5	6	7	8	9	10	11
	12	11	10	9	8	7	6	5	4	3	2	1	20	1	2	3	4	5	6	7	8	9	10	11	12
	13	12	11	10	9	8	7	6	5	4	3	2	1	2	3	4	5	6	7	8	9	10	11	12	13
	14	13	12	11	10	9	8	7	6	5	4	3	2	1	4	5	6	7	8	9	10	11	12	13	14
	15	14	13	12	11	10	9	8	7	6	5	4	3	2	1	6	7	8	9	10	11	12	13	14	15
	16	15	14	13	12	11	10	9	8	7	6	5	4	3	2	1	8	9	10	11	12	13	14	15	16
	17	16	15	14	13	12	11	10	9	8	7	6	5	4	3	2	1	10	11	12	13	14	15	16	17
	18	17	16	15	14	13	12	11	10	9	8	7	6	5	4	3	2	1	12	13	14	15	16	17	18
	19	18	17	16	15	14	13	12	11	10	9	8	7	6	5	4	3	2	1	14	15	16	17	18	19
	20	19	18	17	16	15	14	13	12	11	10	9	8	7	6	5	4	3	2	1	16	17	18	19	20
	19	20	19	18	17	16	15	14	13	12	11	10	9	8	7	6	5	4	3	2	1	18	19	20	19
	18	19	20	19	18	17	16	15	14	13	12	11	10	9	8	7	6	5	4	3	2	1	20	19	18
	17	18	19	20	19	18	17	16	15	14	13	12	11	10	9	8	7	6	5	4	3	2	1	18	17
	16	17	18	19	20	19	18	17	16	15	14	13	12	11	10	9	8	7	6	5	4	3	2	1	16
	15	16	17	18	19	20	19	18	17	16	15	14	13	12	11	10	9	8	7	6	5	4	3	2	1

SUPERNOVA DESIGN CHART

Bottom half of the quilt. Begin working with Row 25 (far left), which is the outside edge of the quilt and work toward Row 1. Make two of each row and place them next to each outer row so that the design forms a mirror image. Make one of Row 1.

Row number	25	24	23	22	21	20	19	18	17	16	15	14	13	12	11	10	9	8	7	6	5	4	3	2	1
Cut width of rows	2½"	2¾"	3"	2¾"	2½"	2¼"	2"	1¾"	1½"	1¾"	2"	2¼"	2½"	2¾"	3"	3¼"	3½"	3¼"	3"	2¾"	2½"	2¼"	2"	1¾"	1½"
Fabric number	1	2	3	4	1	2	3	4	5	6	7	8	9	10	11	12	13	14	15	16	17	18	19	20	1
	2	1	2	3	2	3	4	5	6	7	8	9	10	11	12	13	14	15	16	17	18	19	20	1	2
	3	2	1	2	3	4	5	6	7	8	9	10	11	12	13	14	15	16	17	18	19	20	1	2	3
	4	3	2	1	4	5	6	7	8	9	10	11	12	13	14	15	16	17	18	19	20	1	2	3	4
	5	4	3	2	1	6	7	8	9	10	11	12	13	14	15	16	17	18	19	20	1	2	3	4	5
	6	5	4	3	2	1	8	9	10	11	12	13	14	15	16	17	18	19	20	1	2	3	4	5	6
	7	6	5	4	3	2	1	10	11	12	13	14	15	16	17	18	19	20	1	2	3	4	5	6	7
	8	7	6	5	4	3	2	1	12	13	14	15	16	17	18	19	20	1	2	3	4	5	6	7	8
	9	8	7	6	5	4	3	2	1	14	15	16	17	18	19	20	1	2	3	4	5	6	7	8	9
	10	9	8	7	6	5	4	3	2	1	16	17	18	19	20	1	2	3	4	5	6	7	8	9	10
	11	10	9	8	7	6	5	4	3	2	1	18	19	20	1	2	3	4	5	6	7	8	9	10	11
	12	11	10	9	8	7	6	5	4	3	2	1	20	1	2	3	4	5	6	7	8	9	10	11	12
	13	12	11	10	9	8	7	6	5	4	3	2	1	2	3	4	5	6	7	8	9	10	11	12	13
	14	13	12	11	10	9	8	7	6	5	4	3	2	1	4	5	6	7	8	9	10	11	12	13	14
	15	14	13	12	11	10	9	8	7	6	5	4	3	2	1	6	7	8	9	10	11	12	13	14	15
	16	15	14	13	12	11	10	9	8	7	6	5	4	3	2	1	8	9	10	11	12	13	14	15	16
	17	16	15	14	13	12	11	10	9	8	7	6	5	4	3	2	1	10	11	12	13	14	15	16	17
	18	17	16	15	14	13	12	11	10	9	8	7	6	5	4	3	2	1	12	13	14	15	16	17	18
	19	18	17	16	15	14	13	12	11	10	9	8	7	6	5	4	3	2	1	14	15	16	17	18	19
	20	19	18	17	16	15	14	13	12	11	10	9	8	7	6	5	4	3	2	1	16	17	18	19	20
	19	20	19	18	17	16	15	14	13	12	11	10	9	8	7	6	5	4	3	2	1	18	19	20	19
	18	19	20	19	18	17	16	15	14	13	12	11	10	9	8	7	6	5	4	3	2	1	20	19	18
	17	18	19	20	19	18	17	16	15	14	13	12	11	10	9	8	7	6	5	4	3	2	1	18	17
	16	17	18	19	20	19	18	17	16	15	14	13	12	11	10	9	8	7	6	5	4	3	2	1	16

QUALICUM ZEPHYR

This little wall quilt almost didn't happen because finding 30 perfect fabrics for this out-of-the-box design was just a bit daunting—even for me. But when I stumbled across a gradated fabric in one color range that transitioned gradually from light to dark, I saw how I could use it to make my concept work. My friend Gail Tucker always cuts her strips from the lengthwise grain of the fabric. That concept used to horrify me, but I realized that by cutting lengthwise strips, I could piece this quilt using only three pieces of gradated fabric. By expanding my thinking a bit, I was able to make this unusual-shaped quilt.

CHOOSING FABRICS

Choose gradated fabrics that stay in the same color range but progress from light to dark across the width of the fabric. You may want to select gradated fabric for the longest and middle ribbons from the same color family and a coordinating color for the shortest ribbon.

MATERIALS

Yardage is based on 42"-wide fabric.

1⅞ yards of gradated fabric for the longest ribbon

1⅜ yards of gradated fabric for the middle ribbon

1 yard of gradated fabric for the shortest ribbon

⅞ yard of dark mottled fabric for background and binding

2 yards of fabric for backing

39" x 63" piece of batting

Finished Size: 31¼" x 54½"

Pieced by author. Nadia Wilson of Port Hardy, British Columbia, Canada,
added her own magic to this quilt with her fabulous machine quilting.

CUTTING

To cut lengthwise strips, align the selvages along one edge and carefully fold your fabric in half lengthwise; then fold the fabric again. Trim off the selvages before cutting the lengthwise strips.

From the gradated fabric for the longest ribbon, cut:

5 strips, 1½" x 60", from the darker area of the *lengthwise* grain (label as fabrics 1–5)

5 strips, 1½" x 60", from the lighter area of the *lengthwise* grain (label as fabrics 6–10)

From the gradated fabric for the middle ribbon, cut:

5 strips, 1½" x 44", from the darker area of the *lengthwise* grain (label as fabrics 1–5)

5 strips, 1½" x 44", from the lighter area of the *lengthwise* grain (label as fabrics 6–10)

For the gradated fabric for the shortest ribbon, cut:

5 strips, 1½" x 30", from the darker area of the *lengthwise* grain (label as fabrics 1–5)

5 strips, 1½" x 30", from the lighter area of the *lengthwise* grain (label as fabrics 6–10)

From the dark mottled fabric for background and binding, cut:

5 binding strips, 2¼" x 42", from the *crosswise* grain

8 strips, 1½" x 42", from the *crosswise* grain

FABRIC MAP

Referring to page 13, use a scrap of each of your bargello fabrics to create a fabric map. You'll need to refer to this map throughout the project in order to position all of your strips correctly to make the design.

MAKING THE STRIP SETS

1. Cut each of the gradated strips in half, so that you have two strips each, 30" long.

2. Referring to "Building Strip Sets" on page 14 and using the five darker strips (fabrics 1–5) for the longest ribbon, sew the strips together in numerical order according to your fabric map to make two identical strip sets. On one strip set, press the seam allowances *up*, toward fabric 1. On the other strip set, press the seam allowances *down*,

toward fabric 5. Cut all odd-number rows from the strip set with the seam allowances pressed up and all even-number rows from the strip set with the seam allowances pressed down.

Make 1 of each.

3. In the same manner, sew the five lighter strips (fabrics 6–10) for the longest ribbon together in numerical order to make two identical strip sets; press the seam allowances as before. You will have a total of four strip sets for the longest ribbon, each about 30" long.

4. Repeat steps 1 and 2 using strips 1–5 and 6–10 for the middle ribbon. You will have a total of four strip sets for the middle ribbon, each about 22" long.

5. In the same manner, make a total of four strip sets using strips 1–5 and 6–10 for the shortest ribbon. Each of these strip sets will be about 15" long.

6. Sew the eight 1½"-wide background strips together to make one strip set. Press the seam allowances in one direction. (The segments from this strip set can be turned upside down when an alternate direction of seam allowances is required.)

LONGEST RIBBON

You'll be working on one ribbon at a time. Each ribbon consists of seven rows. Building each ribbon, and then keeping it on your design wall while you're constructing the next ribbon will make the project easier.

Row 1

1. Using a fabric 1–5 strip set (for the longest ribbon) with the seam allowances pressed up, cut four 1¼"-wide slices. Refer to "Cutting Slices" on page 16 as needed for guidance.

2. Using a fabric 6–10 strip set (for the longest ribbon) with the seam allowances pressed up, cut one 1¼"-wide slice. Remove the stitching between fabrics 6 and 7. Use the single piece of fabric 6 for this row; set aside the remaining segment (fabrics 7–10) for possible use later.

3. From the background strip set, cut five 1¼"-wide slices.

4. On four of the background slices, remove the stitching between the *last* two fabrics to create four segments with seven fabrics each.

5. On the remaining background slice, remove the stitching between two fabrics to create a segment with five fabrics. Set the leftover pieces of background fabrics aside to use later.

6. Using your fabric map and the bold lines on the Qualicum Zephyr Design Chart on page 49 as a guide, sew the segments together in the order indicated on the chart. Rotate the background segments as needed, so that the seam allowances on the background segments are going in the same direction as the ribbon-fabric segments. The numbers assigned to your fabrics should be in the same order as the chart numbers for row 1. You should have 54 fabrics in your row.

7. Check the pressing direction of the entire strip; make sure all the seam allowances are pressed toward the top of the row.

Row 2

1. From a fabric 1–5 strip set with the seam allowances pressed down, cut four 2¼"-wide slices.

2. From a fabric 6–10 strip set with the seam allowances pressed down, cut four 2¼"-wide slices.

3. From the background strip set, cut four 2¼"-wide slices.

4. Referring to your fabric map and using one slice with fabrics 6–10, remove the stitching between fabrics 7 and 8 to make a segment with two fabrics. Repeat to make a total of three segments with two fabrics each. Set aside the remaining three-fabric segment (fabrics 8–10).

5. From the remaining fabric 6–10 slice, remove the stitching between fabrics 8 and 9 to make a segment with three fabrics. Set aside the two-fabric segment (fabrics 9 and 10).

6. On the four background slices, remove the stitching between the fabrics to create four segments with five fabrics, one segment with three fabrics, and one single-fabric piece.

7. Using your fabric map and the chart, sew the segments together in the order indicated on the chart. Rotate the background segments as needed, so that the seam allowances on the background segments are going in the same direction as the ribbon-fabric segments. The numbers assigned to your fabrics should be in the same order as the chart numbers for row 2. You should have 53 fabrics in your row.

8. Check the pressing direction of the entire strip; make sure all the seam allowances are pressed toward the bottom of the row.

Joining the Rows

Sew row 2 to row 1 before assembling row 3.

With right sides together and raw edges aligned, place row 2 on top of row 1. Using a scant ¼"-wide seam allowance, join the rows along their long edges, carefully matching the seam intersections with your finger. You may want to use a stylus or an awl to hold the matched seam intersections in place, gently easing the fabric as needed to align the seams. Press the seam allowances toward row 2.

Row 3

1. From a fabric 1–5 strip set with the seam allowances pressed up, cut four 2¼"-wide slices. From a fabric 6–10 strip set with the seam allowances pressed up, cut four 2¼"-wide slices.

2. From the background strip set, cut one 2¼"-wide slice. Utilize the leftover background segments from row 2 first and then, if needed, cut a second 2¼"-wide slice.

3. In the same manner as before, referring to your fabric map and the chart, remove the stitching between segments, as needed, and join the segments in the order indicated to make row 3. You should have 52 fabrics in the row. Check the pressing direction of the entire strip; make sure all the seam allowances are pressed toward the top of the row.

4. Stitch row 3 to row 2, matching the seam intersections. Press the seam allowances toward row 3.

■ WORKING FROM THE CHART

1. Continue working in the same manner, building one row at a time. Once you have completed rows 1–7 for the longest ribbon, begin a new section with rows 8–14 for the middle ribbon. Refer to your fabric map and the chart to join the segments in the order indicated for the row you are making. Be sure to alternate your cutting between the strip sets so that the odd-number rows (3, 5, 7, etc.) have the seam allowances pressed up and the even-number rows (4, 6, 8, etc) have the seam allowances pressed down.

2. After completing each new row, check that it matches the chart and that the seam allowances are pressed in the correct direction.

3. Join each new row to the section you are constructing and press the seam allowances toward the newly added row.

■ MIDDLE RIBBON AND SHORTEST RIBBON

1. Use the strip sets for the middle ribbon and continue in the same manner as before.

2. Using the chart, count the number of times fabric 1 and fabric 6 are repeated in the row you are building and cut that number of slices from the appropriate strip set. Note that rows 8 and 14 are cut 1¼" wide and rows 9–13 are cut 2¼" wide.

3. From the background strip set, cut one 1¼"-wide slice and one 2¼"-wide slice. Utilize the leftover background segments first and then, if needed, cut a second slice of either width.

4. Repeat steps 2 and 3 using the strip sets for the shortest ribbon. Note that rows 15 and 21 are cut 1¼" wide and rows 16–20 are cut 2¼" wide.

■ ASSEMBLY AND FINISHING

1. Trim the bottom edges of each section at an angle to make a straight edge. Make sure you leave ¼" of fabric past the last seam intersection for seam allowance.

2. Join your three sections in the correct sequence to complete the quilt top. Finish by basting around the quilt top about ⅛" from the outer edges to stabilize the seams for quilting.

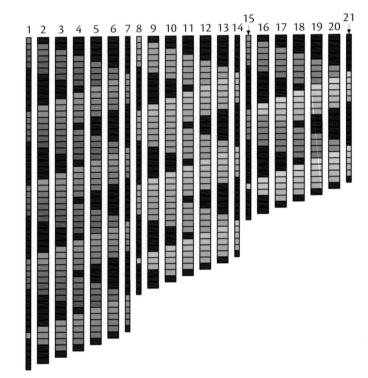

Quilt layout

3. Layer the quilt top with batting and backing. Baste and quilt, referring to pages 92 and 93 as needed. (Or take the neatly folded quilt top and backing to a professional long-arm machine quilter.)

4. If you want to hang your quilt, add a hanging sleeve as described on page 93. Using the 2¼"-wide binding strips and referring to "Binding" on page 94, make and attach the binding.

QUALICUM ZEPHYR DESIGN CHART

The letter B on the chart refers to a strip of background fabric.

	1	2	3	4	5	6	7	8	9	10	11	12	13	14	15	16	17	18	19	20	21
Row number	1	2	3	4	5	6	7	8	9	10	11	12	13	14	15	16	17	18	19	20	21
Cut width of rows	1¼"	2¼"	2¼"	2¼"	2¼"	2¼"	1¼"	1¼"	2¼"	2¼"	2¼"	2¼"	2¼"	2¼"	1¼"	2¼"	2¼"	2¼"	2¼"	2¼"	1¼"
Fabric number	1	B	B	B	B	B	B	1	B	B	B	B	B	B	1	B	B	B	B	B	B
	2	1	B	B	B	B	B	2	1	B	B	B	B	B	2	1	B	B	B	B	B
	3	2	1	B	B	B	B	3	2	1	B	B	B	B	3	2	1	B	B	B	B
	4	3	2	1	B	B	B	4	3	2	1	B	B	B	4	3	2	1	B	B	B
	5	4	3	2	1	B	B	5	4	3	2	1	B	B	5	4	3	2	1	B	B
	B	5	4	3	2	1	B	B	5	4	3	2	1	B	B	5	4	3	2	1	B
	B	B	5	4	3	2	6	B	B	5	4	3	2	6	B	B	5	4	3	2	6
	B	B	B	5	4	6	7	B	B	B	5	4	6	7	B	B	B	5	4	6	7
	B	B	B	6	7	8	9	B	B	B	6	7	8	9	B	B	B	6	7	8	9
	B	B	6	7	8	9	10	B	B	6	7	8	9	10	B	B	6	7	8	9	10
	B	6	7	8	9	10	B	B	6	7	8	9	10	B	B	6	7	8	9	10	B
	1	7	8	9	10	B	B	1	7	8	9	10	B	B	1	7	8	9	10	B	B
	2	1	9	10	B	B	B	2	1	9	10	B	B	B	2	1	9	10	B	B	B
	3	2	1	B	B	B	B	3	2	1	B	B	B	B	3	2	1	B	B	B	B
	4	3	2	1	B	B	B	4	3	2	1	B	B	B	4	3	2	1	B	B	B
	5	4	3	2	1	B	B	5	4	3	2	1	B	B	5	4	3	2	1	B	B
	B	5	4	3	2	1	B	B	5	4	3	2	1	B	B	5	4	3	2	1	B
	B	B	5	4	3	2	6	B	B	5	4	3	2	6	B	B	5	4	3	2	6
	B	B	B	5	4	6	7	B	B	B	5	4	6	7	B	B	B	5	4	6	7
	B	B	B	6	7	8	9	B	B	B	6	7	8	9	B	B	B	6	7	8	9
	B	B	6	7	8	9	10	B	B	6	7	8	9	10	B	B	6	7	8	9	10
	B	6	7	8	9	10	B	B	6	7	8	9	10	B	B	6	7	8	9	10	B
	1	7	8	9	10	B	B	1	7	8	9	10	B	B	6	7	8	9	10	B	
	2	1	9	10	B	B	B	2	1	9	10	B	B	B	B	8	9	10	B		
	3	2	1	B	B	B	B	3	2	1	B	B	B	B	B	B	10	B			
	4	3	2	1	B	B	B	4	3	2	1	B	B	B	B	B	B				
	5	4	3	2	1	B	B	5	4	3	2	1	B	B	B	B					
	B	5	4	3	2	1	B	B	5	4	3	2	1	B	B						
	B	B	5	4	3	2	6	B	B	5	4	3	2	6							
	B	B	B	5	4	6	7	B	B	B	5	4	6	7							
	B	B	B	6	7	8	9	B	B	B	6	7	8	9							
	B	B	6	7	8	9	10	B	B	6	7	8	9	10							
	B	6	7	8	9	10	B	B	6	7	8	9	10	B							
	1	7	8	9	10	B	B	1	7	8	9	10	B	B							
	2	1	9	10	B	B	B	2	1	9	10	B	B	B							
	3	2	1	B	B	B	B	3	2	1	B	B	B	B							
	4	3	2	1	B	B	B	4	3	2	1	B	B	B							
	5	4	3	2	1	B	B	5	4	3	2	1	B	B							
	B	5	4	3	2	1	B	B	5	4	3	2	1	B							
	B	B	5	4	3	2	6	B	B	5	4	3	2	6							
	B	B	B	5	4	6	7	B	B	B	5	4	6	7							
	B	B	B	6	7	8	9	B	B	B	6	7	8	9							
	B	B	6	7	8	9	10	B	B	6	7	8	9	10							
	B	6	7	8	9	10	B	B	6	7	8	9	10	B							
	1	7	8	9	10	B	B	6	7	8	9	10	B								
	2	1	9	10	B	B	B	B	8	9	10	B									
	3	2	1	B	B	B	B	B	B	10	B										
	4	3	2	1	B	B	B	B	B	B											
	5	4	3	2	1	B	B	B	B												
	B	5	4	3	2	1	B	B													
	B	B	5	4	3	2	6														
	B	B	B	5	4	6	7														
	B	B	B	6	7	8	9														
	B	B	6	7	8	9	10														
	B	6	7	8	9	10	B														
	6	7	8	9	10	B															
	B	8	9	10	B																
	B	B	10	B																	
	B	B	B																		
	B	B																			
	B																				

INFINITY

The "Infinity" quilt image danced in my head for a very long time. When I finally drafted it onto graph paper, I realized it would be almost bed size, which just didn't work for me. So I set the idea aside again for a very long time. Then it hit me that instead of stepping the fabrics a full strip (1") each time, I could move them up or down by half a strip width. When I redrafted the quilt using this scale, it worked, creating a suitable wall-sized quilt. Choosing fabrics that glowed for the inside of the ribbon completed my vision for this quilt.

CHOOSING FABRICS

You will need 20 fabrics in one color family, ranging from light to dark. The lightest 10 are for the "inside" of the dancing-ribbon loop. If possible, these colors should have luminescence when placed next to your very dark background fabric. They should light up or almost glow with light.

The other 10 fabrics will be the darker outside of the ribbon. While I always prefer a subtle blend or even gradation between my fabrics, I also try to incorporate one or two zingers that add sparkle.

I used black for my background fabric, but you might like to try navy blue or chocolate brown, depending on your ribbon-color choice. I prefer a background fabric that is almost solid but has some visual texture. These fabrics add more life, depth, and dimension to a project than would a solid-colored fabric.

MATERIALS

Yardage is based on 42"-wide fabric.

¼ yard *each* of 20 fabrics for the bargello ribbon

3 yards of dark fabric for ribbon background, borders, and binding

¼ yard of a bright fabric for border accent

3½ yards of fabric for backing

57" x 67" piece of batting

Finished Size: 50" x 57½"

Pieced by author and beautifully machine quilted by Nadia Wilson of Port Hardy, British Columbia, Canada

CUTTING

From *each* of the 20 fabrics for the bargello ribbon, cut:

3 strips, 1½" x 42"

From the dark fabric for ribbon background, borders, and binding, cut:

7 outer-border strips, 3½" x 42"

5 strips, 2½" x 42"; crosscut 2 *of the strips* into the following lengths:

   4 pieces, 7½" long

   4 pieces, 7" long

6 binding strips, 2¼" x 42"

2 strips, 2" x 42"; crosscut into the following lengths:

   4 pieces, 8" long

   4 pieces, 6½" long

2 strips, 1¾" x 42"; crosscut into the following lengths:

   4 pieces, 8½" long

   4 pieces, 6" long

17 strips, 1½" x 42"; crosscut 3 *of the strips* into the following lengths:

   4 pieces, 9½" long

   4 pieces, 9" long

   4 pieces, 5½" long

   4 pieces, 5" long

3 strips, 1¼" x 42"; crosscut into the following lengths:

   4 pieces, 10½" long

   4 pieces, 10" long

   4 pieces, 4½" long

   4 pieces, 4" long

4 strips, 1" x 42"; crosscut into the following lengths:

   4 pieces, 11½" long

   4 pieces, 11" long

   4 pieces, 3½" long

   4 pieces, 3" long

   2 pieces, 2½" long

From the bright fabric for border accent, cut:

6 strips, 1" x 42"

FABRIC MAP

Referring to page 13, use a scrap of each bargello fabric to create a fabric map; number the light group of fabrics 1–10 and the dark group 11–20. You'll need to refer to your map throughout the project in order to position all of the strips correctly to make the design shown.

MAKING THE STRIP SETS

1. Referring to "Building Strip Sets" on page 14 and using the 10 light bargello fabric strips, sew the strips together in numerical order according to your fabric map to make three identical strip sets. Press the seam allowances toward fabric 10.

2. In the same manner, use the 10 dark bargello fabric strips to make three identical strip sets. Press the seam allowances toward fabric 11.

Fabric 1	Fabric 11
Fabric 2	Fabric 12
Fabric 3	Fabric 13
Fabric 4	Fabric 14
Fabric 5	Fabric 15
Fabric 6	Fabric 16
Fabric 7	Fabric 17
Fabric 8	Fabric 18
Fabric 9	Fabric 19
Fabric 10	Fabric 20

Make 3 of each.

Pressing for Success

When joining the rows, the step up or down will be ½" or half of a strip width, so the seam intersection will not need to match, and the seam allowances will not need to be pressed in opposite directions. In order to create a beautiful project, it is necessary to press all the seam allowances well so that they lie flat.

Thread Color

When using black or another dark background fabric, you may want to use black or a matching thread color for sewing the dark strip sets; then your thread will blend with the fabric and the stitches won't show.

3. Sew eight of the 1½" x 42" background strips together to make one strip set. Press the seam allowances in one direction.

Background-Fabric Strip Set

Why do you need to make a strip set with background-fabric strips instead of using a single strip of fabric cut to the width and length required? The smallest differences in sewing and pressing can affect the length of the piece you're making. Using pieced segments to connect the ribbon slices will make building the rows easier and ensure accuracy. If you use a single strip cut to length on the top and bottom of each row, the outer edges can be trimmed, if needed, before adding the borders.

ROW 1

Row 1 is the middle row of your quilt.

1. From a strip set with fabrics 1–10, cut one 1"-wide slice. Refer to "Cutting Slices" on page 16 as needed for guidance.

2. From a strip set with fabrics 11–20, cut one 1"-wide slice.

3. From a background strip set, cut four 1"-wide slices. On one of the background slices, remove the stitching between two fabrics to create one single fabric piece. Set the seven-fabric segment aside for row 2.

4. With right sides together and using a scant ¼"-wide seam allowance, sew the single fabric piece and the remaining three background slices together to make a 25-piece section.

5. Using the slice with fabrics 1–10, stitch a 1" x 2½" background piece to fabric 10, referring to your fabric map as needed. Fabric 1 will be at the bottom of the row.

6. Sew one end of the background section to fabric 1 at the bottom of the row. Using the slice with fabrics 11–20, stitch fabric 11 to the opposite end of the background section. Then sew a 1" x 2½" background piece to fabric 11 to complete row 1.

7. Using your fabric map as a guide, compare your finished row to row 1 on the Infinity Design Chart on page 57. The numbers assigned to your fabrics should be in the same order as the chart numbers for row 1. Check the pressing direction of the entire strip; make sure all of the seam allowances are pressed in the same direction.

ROW 2

Make two identical rows.

1. From a strip set with fabrics 1–10, cut four 1"-wide slices.

2. From a strip set with fabrics 11–20, cut two 1"-wide slices.

3. From a background strip set, cut three 1"-wide slices. On each slice, remove the stitching between the last two fabrics to make three seven-fabric segments.

4. Use your fabric map as a guide and refer to the Infinity Chart as needed. Using a slice with fabrics 1–10, sew a 1" x 3" background piece to fabric 10 and then sew a seven-fabric background segment to fabric 1.

5. Using another slice with fabrics 1–10, sew fabric 10 to the opposite end of the background segment. Fabric 1 will be at the bottom of the row.

6. Sew a seven-fabric background segment to fabric 1 at the bottom of the row. Using a slice with fabrics 11–20, sew fabric 20 to the opposite end of the background segment. Lastly, sew a 1" x 3" background piece to fabric 11 to complete the row. In the same manner, make a second identical row 2 (using the leftover seven-fabric segment from row 1).

7. Compare the two rows to each other and to the chart for accuracy. Press all seam allowances in the same direction.

8. Lay the rows on your ironing board side by side with row 1 in the middle. They should all be the same length.

Save Time and Money

You may find it will save time and be more economical to build a few rows before pressing. Then heat up your iron and press the seam allowances on several rows, instead of one row at a time.

Stepping Up or Down

Unlike the other quilts in this book, the rows in this quilt are stepped up or down half of the strip width rather than a full strip width. Therefore, there's not a seam intersection to use as a matching point when joining the rows. The seam line of a subsequent row falls at the midpoint of each strip in the previous row.

To create midpoints for matching, fold a row in half every 6 to 8 fabrics and match the seam lines; finger-press to make a crease. When adding the next row, match the seam lines with the center crease on the adjoining row. You may also find that when the new row is wider than the previous row, you can align the seam lines on the new row with the seam lines on a previously sewn row.

Matching up the top and bottom edges can also help to align the rows correctly. For this quilt, I recommend pinning the rows together every 8"–10" before you sew.

JOINING THE ROWS

1. With right sides together and raw edges aligned, place row 2 on top of row 1. Align the top and bottom edges and stagger the seam lines ½" as shown in the quilt layout diagram on page 56. Using a scant ¼"-wide seam allowance, join the rows along their long edges, gently easing the fabric as needed. Press the seam allowances toward the newly added row—away from the quilt center—before sewing the second row 2.

2. Place the second row 2 on top of row 1, right sides together and raw edges aligned. Join the rows along their long edges; see the "Alternate Stitching Direction" box on page 21. Press the seam allowances toward the newly added row.

WORKING FROM THE CHART

1. Continue working in this manner; for each pair of rows cut four slices in the width indicated on the chart from the strip sets with fabrics 1–10 and four slices from the strip sets with fabrics 11–20. Cut two to four slices in the width indicated on the chart from the background strip sets. The number of slices you'll need will depend on the row you are building and how many leftover background segments you can utilize. Referring to your fabric map, remove the stitching between segments, as needed, and join the segments in the order indicated for the row you are making. Each time you'll be making two identical rows.

2. After completing each new pair of rows, check that they match the chart and that they are the same length as the center unit by laying them side by side on your ironing board.

3. Join each new pair of rows to opposite sides of the quilt center, alternating the stitching direction and pressing the seam allowances toward the newly added rows before working on the next pair of rows.

ROW 20

Row 20 is made using the three remaining 2½"-wide background strips. This row allows the bargello ribbon to float on the background.

1. Sew the three strips together using a diagonal seam to make a long strip. Measure the length of the quilt top through the center. Cut two 2½"-wide strips to this length.

2. Lay both strips side by side, in the center of the quilt top. In the seam allowance, use a pencil or chalk marker to mark three or four seam lines as reference points.

3. Pin the borders to the sides of the quilt top, matching the ends and reference points. Sew the borders in place with a ¼"-wide seam allowance, making sure all the seam allowances fall in the intended direction. Press the seam allowances toward the border strips.

BORDERS AND FINISHING

1. Refer to "Borders with Mitered Corners" on page 89 to make a border unit using the remaining 1½"-wide dark background strips, 1"-wide border accent strips, and the 3½"-wide outer-border strips. Measure, cut, and sew the border unit to the quilt top.

2. Layer the quilt top with batting and backing. Baste and quilt, referring to pages 92 and 93 as needed. (Or take the neatly folded quilt top and backing to a professional long-arm machine quilter.)

3. If you want to hang your quilt, add a hanging sleeve as described on page 93. Using the 2¼"-wide binding strips and referring to "Binding" on page 94, make and attach the binding.

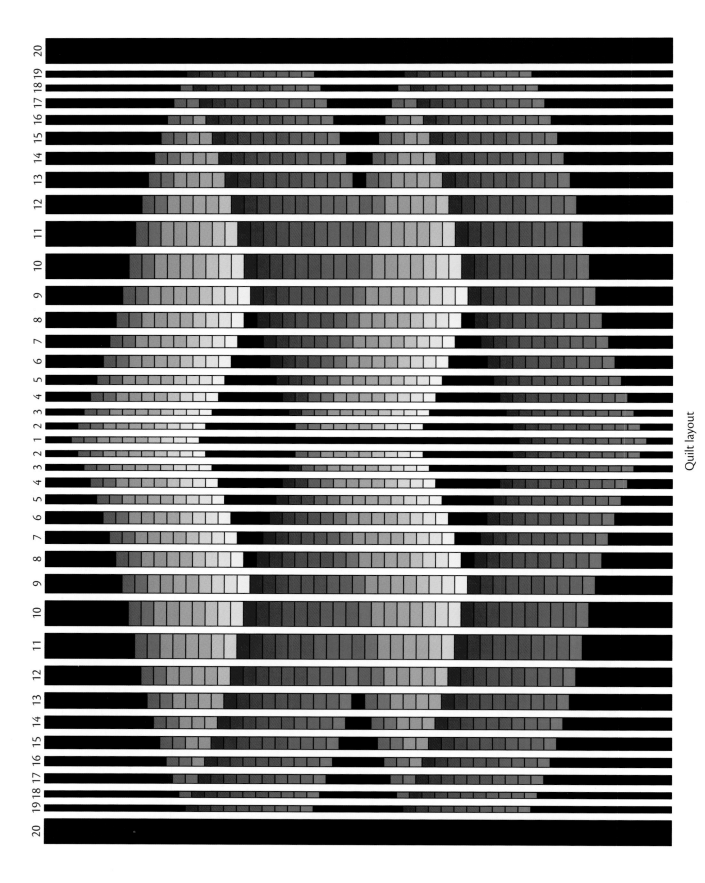

Quilt layout

INFINITY DESIGN CHART

Begin working with Row 1 (far right), which is the center of the quilt. Make two of each subsequent row and place them on either side of the quilt center so that the design forms a mirror image. The letter B on the chart refers to a section of background fabric. Use a single strip in the length indicated at the top and bottom of each row, and use the number of pieces indicated from the background strip set to connect the ribbon slices.

Row number	20	19	18	17	16	15	14	13	12	11	10	9	8	7	6	5	4	3	2	1
Cut width of slices	2½"	1"	1"	1¼"	1¼"	1½"	1½"	1¾"	2"	2½"	2½"	2"	1¾"	1½"	1½"	1¼"	1¼"	1"	1"	1"
Fabric number	B49½"	B11½"	B11"	B10½"	B10"	B9½"	B9"	B8½"	B8"	B7½"	B7"	B6½"	B6"	B5½"	B5"	B4½"	B4"	B3½"	B3"	B2½"
																				10
																			10	9
																		10	9	8
																	10	9	8	7
																10	9	8	7	6
															10	9	8	7	6	5
														10	9	8	7	6	5	4
													10	9	8	7	6	5	4	3
												10	9	8	7	6	5	4	3	2
											10	9	8	7	6	5	4	3	2	1
										10	9	8	7	6	5	4	3	2	1	B25
									10	9	8	7	6	5	4	3	2	1	B7	
								10	9	8	7	6	5	4	3	2	1	B6		
							10	9	8	7	6	5	4	3	2	1	B5			
						10	9	8	7	6	5	4	3	2	1	B4				
					10	9	8	7	6	5	4	3	2	1	B3					
				10	9	8	7	6	5	4	3	2	1	B2						
		20	10	9	8	7	6	5	4	3	2	1	B1							
		19	20																	
		18	19	20																
		17	18	19	20															
		16	17	18	19	20														
		15	16	17	18	19	20													
		14	15	16	17	18	19	20												
		13	14	15	16	17	18	19	20											
		12	13	14	15	16	17	18	19	20										
		11	12	13	14	15	16	17	18	19	20									
		B7	11	12	13	14	15	16	17	18	19	20								
			B6	11	12	13	14	15	16	17	18	19	20							
				B5	11	12	13	14	15	16	17	18	19	20						
					B4	11	12	13	14	15	16	17	18	19	20					
						B3	11	12	13	14	15	16	17	18	19	20				
							B2	11	12	13	14	15	16	17	18	19	20			
								B1	11	12	13	14	15	16	17	18	19	20		
																			10	
																		10	9	
																	10	9	8	
																10	9	8	7	
															10	9	8	7	6	
														10	9	8	7	6	5	
													10	9	8	7	6	5	4	
												10	9	8	7	6	5	4	3	
											10	9	8	7	6	5	4	3	2	
										10	9	8	7	6	5	4	3	2	1	
									10	9	8	7	6	5	4	3	2	1	B7	
								10	9	8	7	6	5	4	3	2	1	B6		
							10	9	8	7	6	5	4	3	2	1	B5			
						10	9	8	7	6	5	4	3	2	1	B4				
					10	9	8	7	6	5	4	3	2	1	B3					
				10	9	8	7	6	5	4	3	2	1	B2						
		20	10	9	8	7	6	5	4	3	2	1	B1							
		19	20																	
		18	19	20																
		17	18	19	20															
		16	17	18	19	20														
		15	16	17	18	19	20													
		14	15	16	17	18	19	20												
		13	14	15	16	17	18	19	20											
		12	13	14	15	16	17	18	19	20										
		11	12	13	14	15	16	17	18	19	20									
		B11½"	11	12	13	14	15	16	17	18	19	20								
			B11"	11	12	13	14	15	16	17	18	19	20							
				B10½"	11	12	13	14	15	16	17	18	19	20						
					B10"	11	12	13	14	15	16	17	18	19	20					
						B9½"	11	12	13	14	15	16	17	18	19	20				
							B9"	11	12	13	14	15	16	17	18	19	20			
								B8½"	11	12	13	14	15	16	17	18	19	20		
									B8"	11	12	13	14	15	16	17	18	19	20	
										B7½"	11	12	13	14	15	16	17	18	19	20
											B7"	11	12	13	14	15	16	17	18	19
												B6½"	11	12	13	14	15	16	17	18
													B6"	11	12	13	14	15	16	17
														B5½"	11	12	13	14	15	16
															B5"	11	12	13	14	15
																B4½"	11	12	13	14
																	B4"	11	12	13
																		B3½"	11	12
																			B3"	11
																				B2½"

NEBULA

Nebula is my attempt to replicate the fireworks I used to watch from the comfort of my living room before fireworks were made illegal in Nanaimo. My little condo is just high enough to have an unobstructed view of the area where city celebrations were always held. I always thought that those bright explosions of vibrant color would make a fun and exciting wall quilt. Doesn't it make you think of the Fourth of July?

CHOOSING FABRICS

You will need a total of 20 fabrics in two groups: a light group of 10 fabrics (yellow to orange) and a dark group of 10 fabrics (dark orange to red). A fairly even gradation of values will add to the overall effect of this quilt.

Fringe Benefit

The fabrics in this quilt are not used in equal amounts; you'll use more of the light group of fabrics than the dark group. You'll also end up with an unusually large number of leftover bits. The leftover bits can easily be sewn into nine-patch units that finish at 4½". These units can be sewn together to make a cheerful comfort quilt for a child.

MATERIALS

Yardage is based on 42"-wide fabric.

½ yard *each* of 10 lighter bargello fabrics

⅓ yard *each* of 10 darker bargello fabrics

⅝ yard of a dark fabric for binding

4 yards of fabric for backing

67" x 67" piece of batting

Finished Size: 59" x 59"

Pieced by author and machine quilted by Nadia Wilson of Port Hardy, British Columbia, Canada

CUTTING

From *each* of the 10 lighter bargello fabrics, cut:
7 strips, 2" x 42"*

From *each* of the 10 darker bargello fabrics, cut:
4 strips, 2" x 42"

From the dark fabric for binding fabric, cut:
7 strips, 2¼" x 42"

> *Depending on the width of your strip sets, you may need to cut additional strips from fabrics 7, 8, and 9.*

FABRIC MAP

Referring to page 13, use a scrap of each bargello fabric to create a fabric map; number the light group of fabrics 1 – 10 and the dark group 11 – 20. You'll need to refer to your map throughout the project in order to position all of the strips correctly to make the design shown.

MAKING THE STRIP SETS

1. Referring to "Building Strip Sets" on page 14 and using the 10 light bargello-fabric strips, sew the strips together in numerical order according to your fabric map to make seven identical strip sets. Press the seam allowances toward the even-number fabrics.

2. In the same manner, use the 10 dark bargello fabric strips to make four identical strip sets. Press the seam allowances toward the even-number fabrics.

Fabric 1		Fabric 11
Fabric 2		Fabric 12
Fabric 3		Fabric 13
Fabric 4		Fabric 14
Fabric 5		Fabric 15
Fabric 6		Fabric 16
Fabric 7		Fabric 17
Fabric 8		Fabric 18
Fabric 9		Fabric 19
Fabric 10		Fabric 20

Make 7 strip sets.   Make 4 strip sets.

ROW 1

Row 1 is the middle row of your quilt.

1. From a light strip set (fabrics 1 – 10), cut two 1"-wide slices. Refer to "Cutting Slices" on page 16 as needed for guidance.

2. From a dark strip set (fabrics 11 – 20), cut two 1"-wide slices.

3. Referring to your fabric map and using one light slice, remove the stitching between fabrics 1 and 2 to make a segment with fabrics 2 – 10. With right sides together and using a scant ¼"-wide seam allowance, sew fabric 2 to fabric 1 on the remaining fabric 1 – 10 slice to make a 19-piece section for the middle of row 1. Discard the leftover piece or set it aside to use for another project.

4. Using the dark slices, stitch fabric 11 to fabric 10 on each end of the middle section from step 3 to complete row 1.

5. Using your fabric map as a guide, compare your finished row to row 1 on the Nebula Design Chart on page 63. The numbers assigned to your fabrics should be in the same order as the chart numbers for row 1; you should have 39 fabrics in your row. Check the pressing direction of the entire strip; make sure all the seam allowances are pressed toward the even-number fabrics.

ROW 2

Make two identical rows.

1. From a light strip set with fabrics 1 – 10, cut four 1"-wide slices.

2. From a dark strip set with fabrics 11 – 20, cut four 1"-wide slices.

3. Referring to your fabric map and using two of the light slices, remove the stitching between fabrics 1 and 2 to make two segments with fabrics 2 – 10. Sew the single pieces of fabric 1 to fabric 20 on two of the dark slices to make two segments with 11 fabrics each.

4. Using a segment with fabrics 2 – 10 and a segment with 11 fabrics from step 3, sew fabric 10 to fabric 11 to make a section with 20 fabrics. Fabric 2 will now be at the bottom of the row.

5. On the remaining light segment (fabrics 2–10) from step 3, remove the stitching between fabrics 2 and 3. Using the segment with fabrics 3–10, stitch fabric 3 to fabric 2 at the bottom of the row. Discard the leftover piece or set aside to use for another project.

6. Using the remaining 11-fabric segment from step 3, stitch fabric 11 to fabric 10 at the bottom of the row. You now have a complete row. In the same manner, make a second identical row 2.

7. Compare the two rows to each other and to the chart for accuracy. Press all seam allowances in these two rows toward the even-number fabrics.

8. Lay the rows on your ironing board side by side with row 1 in the middle. They should all be the same length and contain 39 pieces of fabric in the number sequence indicated on the chart.

JOINING THE ROWS

Sew a row 2 to either side of row 1 before assembling row 3.

1. With right sides together and raw edges aligned, place row 2 on top of row 1. Using a scant ¼"-wide seam allowance, join the rows along their long edges, carefully matching the seam intersections with your finger. You may want to use a stylus or an awl to hold the matched seam intersections in place, gently easing the fabric as needed to align the seams.

2. Press the seam allowances toward the newly added rows—away from the quilt center—before sewing the second row 2. This center portion of the quilt is the hardest area to press because the center row is only ½" wide when finished. As the quilt top grows larger it becomes much easier to handle.

3. Place the second row 2 on top of row 1, right sides together and raw edges aligned. Join the rows along their long edges, carefully matching the seam intersections. See the "Alternate Stitching Direction" box on page 21.

WORKING FROM THE CHART

1. Continue working in this manner for each pair of rows; from the dark strip sets (fabrics 11–20), cut four slices in the width indicated on the chart for rows 3–19, and two slices for row 20.

2. From the light strips sets (fabrics 1–10), for each pair of rows, you'll need six slices for row 3 and eight slices for rows 4–16 in the width indicated on the chart. For rows 17–20, start by cutting two slices the width indicated on the chart. At this point, you may be able to use some of the leftover segments to complete the rows. (Leftover segments that are too wide can be cut down to the required size.) Referring to your fabric map and using the bold lines on the chart as a guide, remove the stitching between segments, as needed, and join the segments in the order indicated on the chart for the row you are making. Each time you'll be making two identical rows.

3. After completing each new pair of rows, check that they match the chart and that they are the same length as the center unit.

4. Join each new pair of rows to opposite sides of the quilt center, alternating the stitching direction and pressing the seam allowances toward the newly added rows before working on the next pair of rows.

CREATING ADDITIONAL SECTIONS

Once you have completed and added row 10 to each side, you might want to begin two new sections, each with rows 11–20. I find that dividing the project into three sections makes it easier to handle.

1. Continue working in the same manner as described above until you have worked all the way across the chart, adding identical rows to each side of the center. Make sure you have a right side and mirror-image left side that can be joined to the center section.

2. Join the three sections in the correct numerical order to complete the symmetrical design for the quilt.

3. Once all the rows are sewn together, finish by basting around the quilt top about ⅛" from the outer edges to stabilize the seams for quilting.

FINISHING

1. Layer the quilt top with batting and backing. Baste and quilt, referring to pages 92 and 93 as needed. (Or take the neatly folded quilt top and backing to a professional long-arm machine quilter.)

2. If you want to hang your quilt, add a hanging sleeve as described on page 93. Using the 2¼"-wide binding strips and referring to "Binding" on page 94, make and attach the binding.

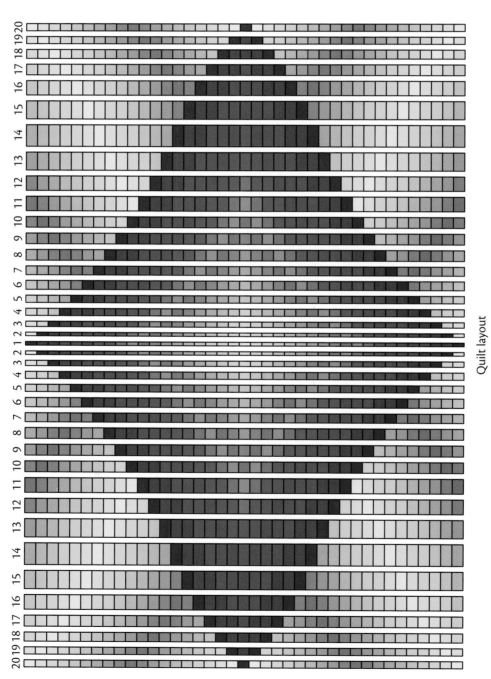

Quilt layout

NEBULA DESIGN CHART

Begin working with Row 1 (far right) in the center of the quilt. Make two of each subsequent row, placing them on either side of the quilt center so that the design forms a mirror image.

Row number	20	19	18	17	16	15	14	13	12	11	10	9	8	7	6	5	4	3	2	1
Cut width of slices	1½"	1½"	1¾"	2"	2½"	3"	3½"	3"	2½"	2½"	2"	2"	2"	1¾"	1¾"	1½"	1½"	1¼"	1"	1"
Fabric number	1	2	3	4	5	6	7	8	9	10	9	8	7	6	5	4	3	2	1	20
	2	1	2	3	4	5	6	7	8	9	10	9	8	7	6	5	4	3	20	19
	3	2	1	2	3	4	5	6	7	8	9	10	9	8	7	6	5	20	19	18
	4	3	2	1	2	3	4	5	6	7	8	9	10	9	8	7	20	19	18	17
	5	4	3	2	1	2	3	4	5	6	7	8	9	10	9	20	19	18	17	16
	6	5	4	3	2	1	2	3	4	5	6	7	8	9	20	19	18	17	16	15
	7	6	5	4	3	2	1	2	3	4	5	6	7	20	19	18	17	16	15	14
	8	7	6	5	4	3	2	1	2	3	4	5	20	19	18	17	16	15	14	13
	9	8	7	6	5	4	3	2	1	2	3	20	19	18	17	16	15	14	13	12
	10	9	8	7	6	5	4	3	2	1	20	19	18	17	16	15	14	13	12	11
	9	10	9	8	7	6	5	4	3	20	19	18	17	16	15	14	13	12	11	10
	8	9	10	9	8	7	6	5	20	19	18	17	16	15	14	13	12	11	10	9
	7	8	9	10	9	8	7	20	19	18	17	16	15	14	13	12	11	10	9	8
	6	7	8	9	10	9	20	19	18	17	16	15	14	13	12	11	10	9	8	7
	5	6	7	8	9	20	19	18	17	16	15	14	13	12	11	10	9	8	7	6
	4	5	6	7	20	19	18	17	16	15	14	13	12	11	10	9	8	7	6	5
	3	4	5	20	19	18	17	16	15	14	13	12	11	10	9	8	7	6	5	4
	2	3	20	19	18	17	16	15	14	13	12	11	10	9	8	7	6	5	4	3
	1	20	19	18	17	16	15	14	13	12	11	10	9	8	7	6	5	4	3	2
	20	19	18	17	16	15	14	13	12	11	10	9	8	7	6	5	4	3	2	1
	1	20	19	18	17	16	15	14	13	12	11	10	9	8	7	6	5	4	3	2
	2	3	20	19	18	17	16	15	14	13	12	11	10	9	8	7	6	5	4	3
	3	4	5	20	19	18	17	16	15	14	13	12	11	10	9	8	7	6	5	4
	4	5	6	7	20	19	18	17	16	15	14	13	12	11	10	9	8	7	6	5
	5	6	7	8	9	20	19	18	17	16	15	14	13	12	11	10	9	8	7	6
	6	7	8	9	10	9	20	19	18	17	16	15	14	13	12	11	10	9	8	7
	7	8	9	10	9	8	7	20	19	18	17	16	15	14	13	12	11	10	9	8
	8	9	10	9	8	7	6	5	20	19	18	17	16	15	14	13	12	11	10	9
	9	10	9	8	7	6	5	4	3	20	19	18	17	16	15	14	13	12	11	10
	10	9	8	7	6	5	4	3	2	1	20	19	18	17	16	15	14	13	12	11
	9	8	7	6	5	4	3	2	1	2	3	20	19	18	17	16	15	14	13	12
	8	7	6	5	4	3	2	1	2	3	4	5	20	19	18	17	16	15	14	13
	7	6	5	4	3	2	1	2	3	4	5	6	7	20	19	18	17	16	15	14
	6	5	4	3	2	1	2	3	4	5	6	7	8	9	20	19	18	17	16	15
	5	4	3	2	1	2	3	4	5	6	7	8	9	10	9	20	19	18	17	16
	4	3	2	1	2	3	4	5	6	7	8	9	10	9	8	7	20	19	18	17
	3	2	1	2	3	4	5	6	7	8	9	10	9	8	7	6	5	20	19	18
	2	1	2	3	4	5	6	7	8	9	10	9	8	7	6	5	4	3	20	19
	1	2	3	4	5	6	7	8	9	10	9	8	7	6	5	4	3	2	1	20

SURF SONG

"Surf Song" is one of my favorite quilts in this book. I originally designed it as a lap quilt, but I liked it so much I redesigned the quilt to include 24 fabrics instead of just 20, so I could make a bed-sized version. Blue has always been my favorite color, and I had been trying for ages to make a blue and emerald green quilt but always seemed to end up with a collection of fabrics that was more blue and purple. I guess I must secretly like purple too!

CHOOSING FABRICS

This quilt uses 24 fabrics in two color groups: 16 fabrics in your main color group (I used blue) and 8 in a similar color group (I used blue-green). Fabrics in each color group should range from light to dark.

MATERIALS

Yardage is based on 42"-wide fabric.

⅝ yard *each* of 24 bargello fabrics

⅞ yard of a dark fabric for binding

9½ yards of fabric for backing

104" x 106" piece of batting

CUTTING

From *each* of the 24 bargello fabrics, cut:

7 strips, 2½" x 42"

From the dark fabric for binding, cut:

11 strips, 2¼" x 42"

FABRIC MAP

Referring to page 13, use a scrap of each of your bargello fabrics to create a fabric map. You'll need to refer to your map throughout the project in order to position all of your strips correctly to make the design shown. For the quilt on page 65, fabric 1 is the lightest blue-green fabric and fabric 9 is the lightest blue fabric.

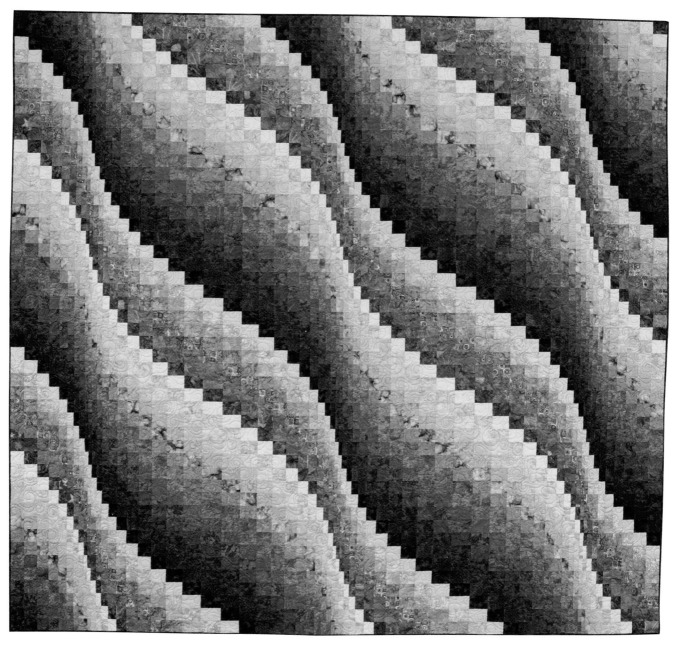

Finished Size: 98" x 96½"

Pieced by author and machine quilted by Pat and Don Bays of Nanaimo, British Columbia, Canada

■ MAKING THE STRIP SETS

Referring to "Building Strip Sets" on page 14 and using the 2½"-wide bargello fabric strips, sew the strips together in numerical order according to your fabric map to make seven identical strip sets. Press all seam allowances toward the even-number fabric strips.

Fabric 1
Fabric 2
Fabric 3
Fabric 4
Fabric 5
Fabric 6
Fabric 7
Fabric 8
Fabric 9
Fabric 10
Fabric 11
Fabric 12
Fabric 13
Fabric 14
Fabric 15
Fabric 16
Fabric 17
Fabric 18
Fabric 19
Fabric 20
Fabric 21
Fabric 22
Fabric 23
Fabric 24

Make 7 strip sets.

Sew Easy

This asymmetrical quilt is easier to make than some of the other projects in this book and you won't have any leftover bits and pieces. You'll only make one of each row, starting on the far left with row 1 and working to row 64 on the far right. If you have a large design wall, you may want to make a few rows and then pin them to your design wall. That way, you'll have a preview of your quilt before it's finished!

■ ROWS 1 AND 2

1. Referring to "Cutting Slices" on page 16, cut two 2¾"-wide slices for row 1.

2. Sew fabric 1 on the first slice to fabric 24 on the second slice. Then sew the ends (fabrics 1 and 24) together to make a loop. Press both seam allowances toward fabric 24.

3. Turn the fabric loop right side out. Remove the stitching between fabrics 22 and 23. Using your fabric map as a guide, compare your finished row to row 1 on the Surf Song Design Chart on page 68. The numbers assigned to your fabrics should be in the same order as the chart numbers for row 1.

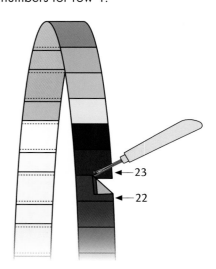

4. Check the pressing direction of the entire strip; make sure all the seam allowances are pressed toward the even-number fabric strips. The row should be 96½" long.

5. For row 2, cut two 2½"-wide slices. Repeat steps 2–4, removing the stitching between fabrics 21 and 22, and then compare the completed row to row 2 on the chart.

JOINING THE ROWS

With right sides together and raw edges aligned, place row 2 on top of row 1. Using a scant ¼"-wide seam allowance, join the rows along their long edges, carefully matching the seam intersections with your finger. You may want to use a stylus or an awl to hold the matched seam intersections in place, gently easing the fabric as needed to align the seams. Press the seam allowances toward row 2, and then each newly added subsequent row.

WORKING FROM THE CHART

1. Continue working in the same manner, cutting two slices in the width indicated on the chart and building one row at a time. Referring to your fabric map and using the bold lines on the chart as a guide, remove the stitching between segments, as needed, and join the segments in the order indicated for the row you are making. Once you have completed 16 rows, you might want to begin a new section with rows 17–32; then build two additional sections for rows 33–48 and rows 49–64. Dividing the project into four sections makes it easier to handle.

2. After completing each new row, check that it matches the chart and that the seam allowances are pressed toward the even-number fabric strips.

3. Join each new row to the section you are constructing and press the seam allowances toward the newly added row.

Make Mine King Size

If you want a larger quilt, simply add a border, and you will have a king-size quilt. A 6"-wide border on each side will make this quilt about 108" x 110", which is a generous king size.

ASSEMBLY

1. Join the four sections in the correct numerical order to complete the center of your quilt top.

2. Once all the sections are sewn together, finish by basting around the quilt top about ⅛" from the outer edges to stabilize the seams for quilting.

FINISHING

1. Layer the quilt top with batting and backing. Baste and quilt, referring to pages 92 and 93 as needed. (Or take the neatly folded quilt top and backing to a professional long-arm machine quilter.)

2. If you want to hang your quilt, add a hanging sleeve as described on page 93. Using the 2¼"-wide binding strips and referring to "Binding" on page 94, make and attach the binding.

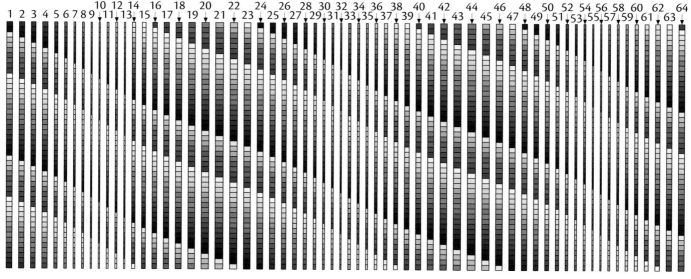

Quilt layout

SURF SONG DESIGN CHART

Begin working with Row 1 to make the left half of the quilt.

Row number	1	2	3	4	5	6	7	8	9	10	11	12	13	14	15	16	17	18	19	20	21	22	23	24	25	26	27	28	29	30	31	32
Cut width of slices	2¾"	2½"	2¼"	2"	1¾"	1½"	1¼"	1¼"	1"	1"	1¼"	1¼"	1½"	1¾"	2"	2¼"	2½"	2¾"	3"	3¼"	3½"	3¼"	3"	2¾"	2½"	2¼"	2"	1¾"	1½"	1¼"	1¼"	1"
Fabric number	23	22	21	20	19	18	17	16	15	14	13	12	11	10	9	8	7	6	5	4	3	2	1	24	23	22	21	20	19	18	17	16
	24	23	22	21	20	19	18	17	16	15	14	13	12	11	10	9	8	7	6	5	4	3	2	1	24	23	22	21	20	19	18	17
	1	24	23	22	21	20	19	18	17	16	15	14	13	12	11	10	9	8	7	6	5	4	3	2	1	24	23	22	21	20	19	18
	2	1	24	23	22	21	20	19	18	17	16	15	14	13	12	11	10	9	8	7	6	5	4	3	2	1	24	23	22	21	20	19
	3	2	1	24	23	22	21	20	19	18	17	16	15	14	13	12	11	10	9	8	7	6	5	4	3	2	1	24	23	22	21	20
	4	3	2	1	24	23	22	21	20	19	18	17	16	15	14	13	12	11	10	9	8	7	6	5	4	3	2	1	24	23	22	21
	5	4	3	2	1	24	23	22	21	20	19	18	17	16	15	14	13	12	11	10	9	8	7	6	5	4	3	2	1	24	23	22
	6	5	4	3	2	1	24	23	22	21	20	19	18	17	16	15	14	13	12	11	10	9	8	7	6	5	4	3	2	1	24	23
	7	6	5	4	3	2	1	24	23	22	21	20	19	18	17	16	15	14	13	12	11	10	9	8	7	6	5	4	3	2	1	24
	8	7	6	5	4	3	2	1	24	23	22	21	20	19	18	17	16	15	14	13	12	11	10	9	8	7	6	5	4	3	2	1
	9	8	7	6	5	4	3	2	1	24	23	22	21	20	19	18	17	16	15	14	13	12	11	10	9	8	7	6	5	4	3	2
	10	9	8	7	6	5	4	3	2	1	24	23	22	21	20	19	18	17	16	15	14	13	12	11	10	9	8	7	6	5	4	3
	11	10	9	8	7	6	5	4	3	2	1	24	23	22	21	20	19	18	17	16	15	14	13	12	11	10	9	8	7	6	5	4
	12	11	10	9	8	7	6	5	4	3	2	1	24	23	22	21	20	19	18	17	16	15	14	13	12	11	10	9	8	7	6	5
	13	12	11	10	9	8	7	6	5	4	3	2	1	24	23	22	21	20	19	18	17	16	15	14	13	12	11	10	9	8	7	6
	14	13	12	11	10	9	8	7	6	5	4	3	2	1	24	23	22	21	20	19	18	17	16	15	14	13	12	11	10	9	8	7
	15	14	13	12	11	10	9	8	7	6	5	4	3	2	1	24	23	22	21	20	19	18	17	16	15	14	13	12	11	10	9	8
	16	15	14	13	12	11	10	9	8	7	6	5	4	3	2	1	24	23	22	21	20	19	18	17	16	15	14	13	12	11	10	9
	17	16	15	14	13	12	11	10	9	8	7	6	5	4	3	2	1	24	23	22	21	20	19	18	17	16	15	14	13	12	11	10
	18	17	16	15	14	13	12	11	10	9	8	7	6	5	4	3	2	1	24	23	22	21	20	19	18	17	16	15	14	13	12	11
	19	18	17	16	15	14	13	12	11	10	9	8	7	6	5	4	3	2	1	24	23	22	21	20	19	18	17	16	15	14	13	12
	20	19	18	17	16	15	14	13	12	11	10	9	8	7	6	5	4	3	2	1	24	23	22	21	20	19	18	17	16	15	14	13
	21	20	19	18	17	16	15	14	13	12	11	10	9	8	7	6	5	4	3	2	1	24	23	22	21	20	19	18	17	16	15	14
	22	21	20	19	18	17	16	15	14	13	12	11	10	9	8	7	6	5	4	3	2	1	24	23	22	21	20	19	18	17	16	15
	23	22	21	20	19	18	17	16	15	14	13	12	11	10	9	8	7	6	5	4	3	2	1	24	23	22	21	20	19	18	17	16
	24	23	22	21	20	19	18	17	16	15	14	13	12	11	10	9	8	7	6	5	4	3	2	1	24	23	22	21	20	19	18	17
	1	24	23	22	21	20	19	18	17	16	15	14	13	12	11	10	9	8	7	6	5	4	3	2	1	24	23	22	21	20	19	18
	2	1	24	23	22	21	20	19	18	17	16	15	14	13	12	11	10	9	8	7	6	5	4	3	2	1	24	23	22	21	20	19
	3	2	1	24	23	22	21	20	19	18	17	16	15	14	13	12	11	10	9	8	7	6	5	4	3	2	1	24	23	22	21	20
	4	3	2	1	24	23	22	21	20	19	18	17	16	15	14	13	12	11	10	9	8	7	6	5	4	3	2	1	24	23	22	21
	5	4	3	2	1	24	23	22	21	20	19	18	17	16	15	14	13	12	11	10	9	8	7	6	5	4	3	2	1	24	23	22
	6	5	4	3	2	1	24	23	22	21	20	19	18	17	16	15	14	13	12	11	10	9	8	7	6	5	4	3	2	1	24	23
	7	6	5	4	3	2	1	24	23	22	21	20	19	18	17	16	15	14	13	12	11	10	9	8	7	6	5	4	3	2	1	24
	8	7	6	5	4	3	2	1	24	23	22	21	20	19	18	17	16	15	14	13	12	11	10	9	8	7	6	5	4	3	2	1
	9	8	7	6	5	4	3	2	1	24	23	22	21	20	19	18	17	16	15	14	13	12	11	10	9	8	7	6	5	4	3	2
	10	9	8	7	6	5	4	3	2	1	24	23	22	21	20	19	18	17	16	15	14	13	12	11	10	9	8	7	6	5	4	3
	11	10	9	8	7	6	5	4	3	2	1	24	23	22	21	20	19	18	17	16	15	14	13	12	11	10	9	8	7	6	5	4
	12	11	10	9	8	7	6	5	4	3	2	1	24	23	22	21	20	19	18	17	16	15	14	13	12	11	10	9	8	7	6	5
	13	12	11	10	9	8	7	6	5	4	3	2	1	24	23	22	21	20	19	18	17	16	15	14	13	12	11	10	9	8	7	6
	14	13	12	11	10	9	8	7	6	5	4	3	2	1	24	23	22	21	20	19	18	17	16	15	14	13	12	11	10	9	8	7
	15	14	13	12	11	10	9	8	7	6	5	4	3	2	1	24	23	22	21	20	19	18	17	16	15	14	13	12	11	10	9	8
	16	15	14	13	12	11	10	9	8	7	6	5	4	3	2	1	24	23	22	21	20	19	18	17	16	15	14	13	12	11	10	9
	17	16	15	14	13	12	11	10	9	8	7	6	5	4	3	2	1	24	23	22	21	20	19	18	17	16	15	14	13	12	11	10
	18	17	16	15	14	13	12	11	10	9	8	7	6	5	4	3	2	1	24	23	22	21	20	19	18	17	16	15	14	13	12	11
	19	18	17	16	15	14	13	12	11	10	9	8	7	6	5	4	3	2	1	24	23	22	21	20	19	18	17	16	15	14	13	12
	20	19	18	17	16	15	14	13	12	11	10	9	8	7	6	5	4	3	2	1	24	23	22	21	20	19	18	17	16	15	14	13
	21	20	19	18	17	16	15	14	13	12	11	10	9	8	7	6	5	4	3	2	1	24	23	22	21	20	19	18	17	16	15	14
	22	21	20	19	18	17	16	15	14	13	12	11	10	9	8	7	6	5	4	3	2	1	24	23	22	21	20	19	18	17	16	15

SURF SONG DESIGN CHART

Begin working in the center of the design with Row 33 to make the right half of the quilt.

Row number	33	34	35	36	37	38	39	40	41	42	43	44	45	46	47	48	49	50	51	52	53	54	55	56	57	58	59	60	61	62	63	64
Cut width of slices	1"	1¼"	1¼"	1½"	1¾"	2"	2¼"	2½"	2¾"	3"	3¼"	3½"	3¼"	3"	2¾"	2½"	2¼"	2"	1¾"	1½"	1¼"	1¼"	1"	1"	1¼"	1¼"	1½"	1¾"	2"	2¼"	2½"	2¾"
Fabric number	15	14	13	12	11	10	9	8	7	6	5	4	3	2	1	24	23	22	21	20	19	18	17	16	15	14	13	12	11	10	9	8
	16	15	14	13	12	11	10	9	8	7	6	5	4	3	2	1	24	23	21	21	20	19	18	17	16	15	14	13	12	11	10	9
	17	16	15	14	13	12	11	10	9	8	7	6	5	4	3	2	1	24	23	22	21	20	19	18	17	16	15	14	13	12	11	10
	18	17	16	15	14	13	12	11	10	9	8	7	6	5	4	3	2	1	24	23	22	21	20	19	18	17	16	15	14	13	12	11
	19	18	17	16	15	14	13	12	11	10	9	8	7	6	5	4	3	2	1	24	23	22	21	20	19	18	17	16	15	14	13	12
	20	19	18	17	16	15	14	13	12	11	10	9	8	7	6	5	4	3	2	1	24	23	22	21	20	19	18	17	16	15	14	13
	21	20	19	18	17	16	15	14	13	12	11	10	9	8	7	6	5	4	3	2	1	24	23	22	21	20	19	18	17	16	15	14
	22	21	20	19	18	17	16	15	14	13	12	11	10	9	8	7	6	5	4	3	2	1	24	23	22	21	20	19	18	17	16	15
	23	22	21	20	19	18	17	16	15	14	13	12	11	10	9	8	7	6	5	4	3	2	1	24	23	22	21	20	19	18	17	16
	24	23	22	21	20	19	18	17	16	15	14	13	12	11	10	9	8	7	6	5	4	3	2	1	24	23	22	21	20	19	18	17
	1	24	23	22	21	20	19	18	17	16	15	14	13	12	11	10	9	8	7	6	5	4	3	2	1	24	23	22	21	20	19	18
	2	1	24	23	22	21	20	19	18	17	16	15	14	13	12	11	10	9	8	7	6	5	4	3	2	1	24	23	22	21	20	19
	3	2	1	24	23	22	21	20	19	18	17	16	15	14	13	12	11	10	9	8	7	6	5	4	3	2	1	24	23	22	21	20
	4	3	2	1	24	23	22	21	20	19	18	17	16	15	14	13	12	11	10	9	8	7	6	5	4	3	2	1	24	23	22	21
	5	4	3	2	1	24	23	22	21	20	19	18	17	16	15	14	13	12	11	10	9	8	7	6	5	4	3	2	1	24	23	22
	6	5	4	3	2	1	24	23	22	21	20	19	18	17	16	15	14	13	12	11	10	9	8	7	6	5	4	3	2	1	24	23
	7	6	5	4	3	2	1	24	23	22	21	20	19	18	17	16	15	14	13	12	11	10	9	8	7	6	5	4	3	2	1	24
	8	7	6	5	4	3	2	1	24	23	22	21	20	19	18	17	16	15	14	13	12	11	10	9	8	7	6	5	4	3	2	1
	9	8	7	6	5	4	3	2	1	24	23	22	21	20	19	18	17	16	15	14	13	12	11	10	9	8	7	6	5	4	3	2
	10	9	8	7	6	5	4	3	2	1	24	23	22	21	20	19	18	17	16	15	14	13	12	11	10	9	8	7	6	5	4	3
	11	10	9	8	7	6	5	4	3	2	1	24	23	22	21	20	19	18	17	16	15	14	13	12	11	10	9	8	7	6	5	4
	12	11	10	9	8	7	6	5	4	3	2	1	24	23	22	21	20	19	18	17	16	15	14	13	12	11	10	9	8	7	6	5
	13	12	11	10	9	8	7	6	5	4	3	2	1	24	23	22	21	20	19	18	17	16	15	14	13	12	11	10	9	8	7	6
	14	13	12	11	10	9	8	7	6	5	4	3	2	1	24	23	22	21	20	19	18	17	16	15	14	13	12	11	10	9	8	7
	15	14	13	12	11	10	9	8	7	6	5	4	3	2	1	24	23	22	21	20	19	18	17	16	15	14	13	12	11	10	9	8
	16	15	14	13	12	11	10	9	8	7	6	5	4	3	2	1	24	23	22	21	20	19	18	17	16	15	14	13	12	11	10	9
	17	16	15	14	13	12	11	10	9	8	7	6	5	4	3	2	1	24	23	22	21	20	19	18	17	16	15	14	13	12	11	10
	18	17	16	15	14	13	12	11	10	9	8	7	6	5	4	3	2	1	24	23	22	21	20	19	18	17	16	15	14	13	12	11
	19	18	17	16	15	14	13	12	11	10	9	8	7	6	5	4	3	2	1	24	23	22	21	20	19	18	17	16	15	14	13	12
	20	19	18	17	16	15	14	13	12	11	10	9	8	7	6	5	4	3	2	1	24	23	22	21	20	19	18	17	16	15	14	13
	21	20	19	18	17	16	15	14	13	12	11	10	9	8	7	6	5	4	3	2	1	24	23	22	21	20	19	18	17	16	15	14
	22	21	20	19	18	17	16	15	14	13	12	11	10	9	8	7	6	5	4	3	2	1	24	23	22	21	20	19	18	17	16	15
	23	22	21	20	19	18	17	16	15	14	13	12	11	10	9	8	7	6	5	4	3	2	1	24	23	22	21	20	19	18	17	16
	24	23	22	21	20	19	18	17	16	15	14	13	12	11	10	9	8	7	6	5	4	3	2	1	24	23	22	21	20	19	18	17
	1	24	23	22	21	20	19	18	17	16	15	14	13	12	11	10	9	8	7	6	5	4	3	2	1	24	23	22	21	20	19	18
	2	1	24	23	22	21	20	19	18	17	16	15	14	13	12	11	10	9	8	7	6	5	4	3	2	1	24	23	22	21	20	19
	3	2	1	24	23	22	21	20	19	18	17	16	15	14	13	12	11	10	9	8	7	6	5	4	3	2	1	24	23	22	21	20
	4	3	2	1	24	23	22	21	20	19	18	17	16	15	14	13	12	11	10	9	8	7	6	5	4	3	2	1	24	23	22	21
	5	4	3	2	1	24	23	22	21	20	19	18	17	16	15	14	13	12	11	10	9	8	7	6	5	4	3	2	1	24	23	22
	6	5	4	3	2	1	24	23	22	21	20	19	18	17	16	15	14	13	12	11	10	9	8	7	6	5	4	3	2	1	24	23
	7	6	5	4	3	2	1	24	23	22	21	20	19	18	17	16	15	14	13	12	11	10	9	8	7	6	5	4	3	2	1	24
	8	7	6	5	4	3	2	1	24	23	22	21	20	19	18	17	16	15	14	13	12	11	10	9	8	7	6	5	4	3	2	1
	9	8	7	6	5	4	3	2	1	24	23	22	21	20	19	18	17	16	15	14	13	12	11	10	9	8	7	6	5	4	3	2
	10	9	8	7	6	5	4	3	2	1	24	23	22	21	20	19	18	17	16	15	14	13	12	11	10	9	8	7	6	5	4	3
	11	10	9	8	7	6	5	4	3	2	1	24	23	22	21	20	19	18	17	16	15	14	13	12	11	10	9	8	7	6	5	4
	12	11	10	9	8	7	6	5	4	3	2	1	24	23	22	21	20	19	18	17	16	15	14	13	12	11	10	9	8	7	6	5
	13	12	11	10	9	8	7	6	5	4	3	2	1	24	23	22	21	20	19	18	17	16	15	14	13	12	11	10	9	8	7	6
	14	13	12	11	10	9	8	7	6	5	4	3	2	1	24	23	22	21	20	19	18	17	16	15	14	13	12	11	10	9	8	7

SURF SONG WALL HANGING

I decided to make this quilt so it could hang on my bedroom wall to match the bed quilt. Both of the "Surf Song" quilts were definitely made just because I really liked them; they use my favorite colors and my favorite inspiration. Having the ocean so close by is part of why I chose to live on Vancouver Island, and these quilts are a constant reminder of the view I cherish. But I have to admit that the inspiration was actually an aerial shot of the Miami shoreline in the opening of the television show *CSI: Miami*, where there are just two gentle waves lapping the shore of the prettiest blue-green water you can imagine.

CHOOSING FABRICS

This quilt uses 20 fabrics in two color groups: 12 fabrics in one color group (blue) and 8 fabrics in a similar color group (blue-green). Fabrics in each color group should range from light to dark.

MATERIALS

Yardage is based on 42"-wide fabric.

¼ yard of *each* of 20 fabrics for bargello

1⅜ yards of a dark fabric for borders and binding

¼ yard of a bright fabric for border accent

3⅜ yards of fabric for backing

55" x 57" piece of batting

CUTTING

From *each* of the 20 fabrics for bargello, cut:
3 strips, 1½" x 42"

From the dark fabric, cut:
6 outer-border strips, 3½" x 42"
6 binding strips, 2¼" x 42"
6 inner-border strips, 1½" x 42"

From the bright fabric for border accent, cut:
6 strips, 1" x 42"

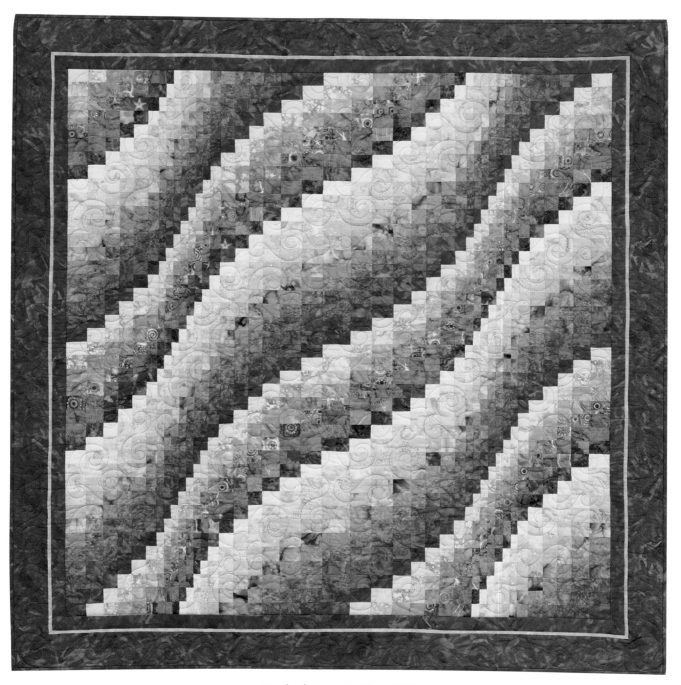

Finished Size: 46½" x 48½"
Pieced by author and machine quilted by Nadia Wilson of Port Hardy, British Columbia, Canada

FABRIC MAP

Referring to page 13, use a scrap of each bargello fabric to create a fabric map. You'll need to refer to your map throughout the project in order to position all of the strips correctly to make the design shown. For the quilt on page 71, fabric 1 is the lightest blue-green fabric and fabric 9 is the lightest blue fabric.

MAKING THE STRIP SETS

Referring to "Building Strip Sets" on page 14 and using the 1½"-wide bargello fabric strips, sew the strips together in numerical order according to your fabric map to make three identical strip sets. Press all seam allowances toward the even-number fabrics.

Fabric 1
Fabric 2
Fabric 3
Fabric 4
Fabric 5
Fabric 6
Fabric 7
Fabric 8
Fabric 9
Fabric 10
Fabric 11
Fabric 12
Fabric 13
Fabric 14
Fabric 15
Fabric 16
Fabric 17
Fabric 18
Fabric 19
Fabric 20

Make 3 strip sets.

ROW 1

1. Referring to "Cutting Slices" on page 16, cut two 2"-wide slices from a strip set.

2. Sew fabric 1 on the first slice to fabric 20 on the second slice. Press both seam allowances toward fabric 20. You now have a complete row.

3. Using your fabric map as a guide, compare your finished row to row 1 on the Surf Song Wall Quilt Design Chart on page 75. The numbers assigned to your fabrics should be in the same order as the chart numbers for row 1. Check the pressing direction of the entire strip; make sure all seam allowances are pressed toward the even-number fabric strips. The row should be 40½" long.

ROW 2

1. From a strip set, cut two 1¾"-wide slices.

2. Sew fabric 1 on the first slice to fabric 20 on the second slice. Then sew the ends (fabrics 1 and 20) together to make a loop. Press both seam allowances toward fabric 20.

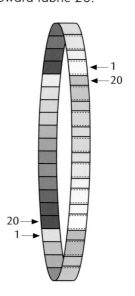

3. Turn the fabric loop right side out. Remove the stitching between fabrics 1 and 2. Using your fabric map as a guide, compare your finished row to row 2 on the chart. The numbers assigned to your fabrics should be in the same order as the chart numbers for row 2.

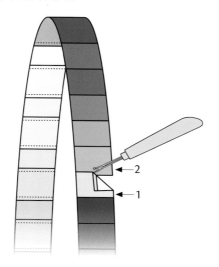

4. Check the pressing direction of the entire strip; make sure all seam allowances are pressed toward the even-number fabric strips.

JOINING THE ROWS

With right sides together and raw edges aligned, place row 2 on top of row 1. Using a scant ¼"-wide seam allowance, join the rows along their long edges, carefully matching the seam intersections with your finger. You may want to use a stylus or an awl to hold the matched seam intersections in place, gently easing the fabric as needed to align the seams. Press the seam allowances toward row 2, and then each newly added subsequent row.

WORKING FROM THE CHART

1. Continue working in the same manner, cutting two slices in the width indicated on the chart and building one row at a time. Referring to your fabric map and using the bold line on the chart as a guide, remove the stitching between segments, as needed, and join the segments in the order indicated for the row you are making. Once you have completed 10 rows, you might want to begin a new section with rows 11–20; then build two additional sections for rows 21–30 and rows 31–41. Dividing the project into four sections makes it easier to handle.

2. After completing each new row, check that it matches the chart and that the seam allowances are pressed toward the even-number fabric strips.

3. Join each new row to the section you are constructing and press the seam allowances toward the newly added row.

4. Join the four sections in the correct numerical order to complete the center of your quilt top.

BORDERS AND FINISHING

1. Refer to "Borders with Mitered Corners" on page 89 to make a border unit using the 1½"-wide inner-border strips, 1"-wide border-accent strips, and the 3½"-wide outer-border strips. Measure, cut, and sew the border unit to the quilt top.

2. Layer the quilt top with batting and backing. Baste and quilt, referring to pages 92 and 93 as needed. (Or take the neatly folded quilt top and backing to a professional long-arm machine quilter.)

3. If you want to hang your quilt, add a hanging sleeve as described on page 93. Using the 2¼"-wide binding strips and referring to "Binding" on page 94, make and attach the binding.

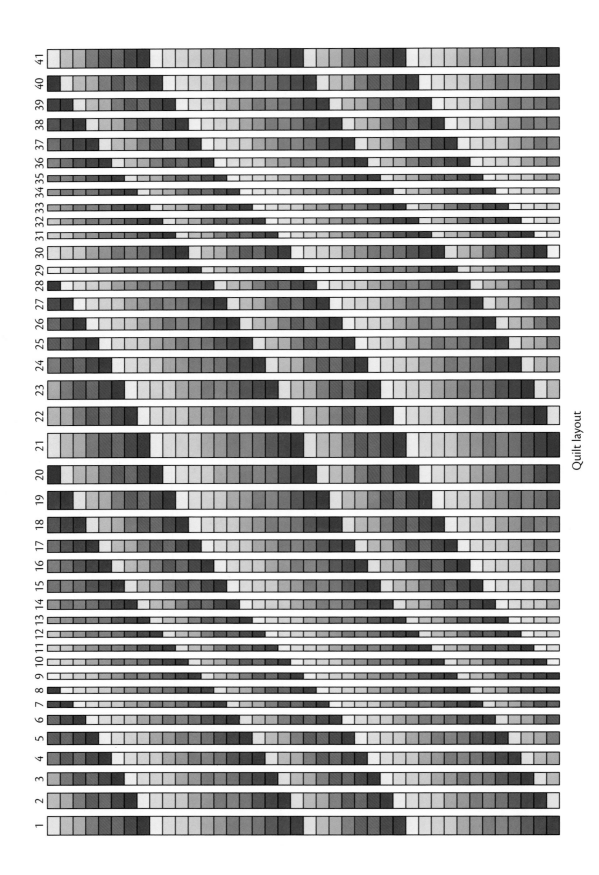

Quilt layout

SURF SONG WALL HANGING DESIGN CHART

Row number	1	2	3	4	5	6	7	8	9	10	11	12	13	14	15	16	17	18	19	20	21	22	23	24	25	26	27	28	29	30	31	32	33	34	35	36	37	38	39	40	41
Cut width of slices	2"	1¾"	1½"	1½"	1½"	1¼"	1"	1"	1"	1"	1"	1"	1"	1¼"	1½"	1½"	1½"	1¾"	2"	2"	2½"	2"	2"	1¾"	1½"	1½"	1½"	1¼"	1"	1"	1"	1"	1"	1"	1"	1¼"	1½"	1½"	1½"	1¾"	2"
Fabric number																																									
1	1	2	3	4	5	6	7	8	9	10	11	12	13	14	15	16	17	18	19	20	1	2	3	4	5	6	7	8	9	10	11	12	13	14	15	16	17	18	19	20	1
2	2	3	4	5	6	7	8	9	10	11	12	13	14	15	16	17	18	19	20	1	2	3	4	5	6	7	8	9	10	11	12	13	14	15	16	17	18	19	20	1	2
3	3	4	5	6	7	8	9	10	11	12	13	14	15	16	17	18	19	20	1	2	3	4	5	6	7	8	9	10	11	12	13	14	15	16	17	18	19	20	1	2	3
4	4	5	6	7	8	9	10	11	12	13	14	15	16	17	18	19	20	1	2	3	4	5	6	7	8	9	10	11	12	13	14	15	16	17	18	19	20	1	2	3	4
5	5	6	7	8	9	10	11	12	13	14	15	16	17	18	19	20	1	2	3	4	5	6	7	8	9	10	11	12	13	14	15	16	17	18	19	20	1	2	3	4	5
6	6	7	8	9	10	11	12	13	14	15	16	17	18	19	20	1	2	3	4	5	6	7	8	9	10	11	12	13	14	15	16	17	18	19	20	1	2	3	4	5	6
7	7	8	9	10	11	12	13	14	15	16	17	18	19	20	1	2	3	4	5	6	7	8	9	10	11	12	13	14	15	16	17	18	19	20	1	2	3	4	5	6	7
8	8	9	10	11	12	13	14	15	16	17	18	19	20	1	2	3	4	5	6	7	8	9	10	11	12	13	14	15	16	17	18	19	20	1	2	3	4	5	6	7	8
9	9	10	11	12	13	14	15	16	17	18	19	20	1	2	3	4	5	6	7	8	9	10	11	12	13	14	15	16	17	18	19	20	1	2	3	4	5	6	7	8	9
10	10	11	12	13	14	15	16	17	18	19	20	1	2	3	4	5	6	7	8	9	10	11	12	13	14	15	16	17	18	19	20	1	2	3	4	5	6	7	8	9	10
11	11	12	13	14	15	16	17	18	19	20	1	2	3	4	5	6	7	8	9	10	11	12	13	14	15	16	17	18	19	20	1	2	3	4	5	6	7	8	9	10	11
12	12	13	14	15	16	17	18	19	20	1	2	3	4	5	6	7	8	9	10	11	12	13	14	15	16	17	18	19	20	1	2	3	4	5	6	7	8	9	10	11	12
13	13	14	15	16	17	18	19	20	1	2	3	4	5	6	7	8	9	10	11	12	13	14	15	16	17	18	19	20	1	2	3	4	5	6	7	8	9	10	11	12	13
14	14	15	16	17	18	19	20	1	2	3	4	5	6	7	8	9	10	11	12	13	14	15	16	17	18	19	20	1	2	3	4	5	6	7	8	9	10	11	12	13	14
15	15	16	17	18	19	20	1	2	3	4	5	6	7	8	9	10	11	12	13	14	15	16	17	18	19	20	1	2	3	4	5	6	7	8	9	10	11	12	13	14	15
16	16	17	18	19	20	1	2	3	4	5	6	7	8	9	10	11	12	13	14	15	16	17	18	19	20	1	2	3	4	5	6	7	8	9	10	11	12	13	14	15	16
17	17	18	19	20	1	2	3	4	5	6	7	8	9	10	11	12	13	14	15	16	17	18	19	20	1	2	3	4	5	6	7	8	9	10	11	12	13	14	15	16	17
18	18	19	20	1	2	3	4	5	6	7	8	9	10	11	12	13	14	15	16	17	18	19	20	1	2	3	4	5	6	7	8	9	10	11	12	13	14	15	16	17	18
19	19	20	1	2	3	4	5	6	7	8	9	10	11	12	13	14	15	16	17	18	19	20	1	2	3	4	5	6	7	8	9	10	11	12	13	14	15	16	17	18	19
20	20	1	2	3	4	5	6	7	8	9	10	11	12	13	14	15	16	17	18	19	20	1	2	3	4	5	6	7	8	9	10	11	12	13	14	15	16	17	18	19	20
1	1	2	3	4	5	6	7	8	9	10	11	12	13	14	15	16	17	18	19	20	1	2	3	4	5	6	7	8	9	10	11	12	13	14	15	16	17	18	19	20	1
2	2	3	4	5	6	7	8	9	10	11	12	13	14	15	16	17	18	19	20	1	2	3	4	5	6	7	8	9	10	11	12	13	14	15	16	17	18	19	20	1	2
3	3	4	5	6	7	8	9	10	11	12	13	14	15	16	17	18	19	20	1	2	3	4	5	6	7	8	9	10	11	12	13	14	15	16	17	18	19	20	1	2	3
4	4	5	6	7	8	9	10	11	12	13	14	15	16	17	18	19	20	1	2	3	4	5	6	7	8	9	10	11	12	13	14	15	16	17	18	19	20	1	2	3	4
5	5	6	7	8	9	10	11	12	13	14	15	16	17	18	19	20	1	2	3	4	5	6	7	8	9	10	11	12	13	14	15	16	17	18	19	20	1	2	3	4	5
6	6	7	8	9	10	11	12	13	14	15	16	17	18	19	20	1	2	3	4	5	6	7	8	9	10	11	12	13	14	15	16	17	18	19	20	1	2	3	4	5	6
7	7	8	9	10	11	12	13	14	15	16	17	18	19	20	1	2	3	4	5	6	7	8	9	10	11	12	13	14	15	16	17	18	19	20	1	2	3	4	5	6	7
8	8	9	10	11	12	13	14	15	16	17	18	19	20	1	2	3	4	5	6	7	8	9	10	11	12	13	14	15	16	17	18	19	20	1	2	3	4	5	6	7	8
9	9	10	11	12	13	14	15	16	17	18	19	20	1	2	3	4	5	6	7	8	9	10	11	12	13	14	15	16	17	18	19	20	1	2	3	4	5	6	7	8	9
10	10	11	12	13	14	15	16	17	18	19	20	1	2	3	4	5	6	7	8	9	10	11	12	13	14	15	16	17	18	19	20	1	2	3	4	5	6	7	8	9	10
11	11	12	13	14	15	16	17	18	19	20	1	2	3	4	5	6	7	8	9	10	11	12	13	14	15	16	17	18	19	20	1	2	3	4	5	6	7	8	9	10	11
12	12	13	14	15	16	17	18	19	20	1	2	3	4	5	6	7	8	9	10	11	12	13	14	15	16	17	18	19	20	1	2	3	4	5	6	7	8	9	10	11	12
13	13	14	15	16	17	18	19	20	1	2	3	4	5	6	7	8	9	10	11	12	13	14	15	16	17	18	19	20	1	2	3	4	5	6	7	8	9	10	11	12	13
14	14	15	16	17	18	19	20	1	2	3	4	5	6	7	8	9	10	11	12	13	14	15	16	17	18	19	20	1	2	3	4	5	6	7	8	9	10	11	12	13	14
15	15	16	17	18	19	20	1	2	3	4	5	6	7	8	9	10	11	12	13	14	15	16	17	18	19	20	1	2	3	4	5	6	7	8	9	10	11	12	13	14	15
16	16	17	18	19	20	1	2	3	4	5	6	7	8	9	10	11	12	13	14	15	16	17	18	19	20	1	2	3	4	5	6	7	8	9	10	11	12	13	14	15	16
17	17	18	19	20	1	2	3	4	5	6	7	8	9	10	11	12	13	14	15	16	17	18	19	20	1	2	3	4	5	6	7	8	9	10	11	12	13	14	15	16	17
18	18	19	20	1	2	3	4	5	6	7	8	9	10	11	12	13	14	15	16	17	18	19	20	1	2	3	4	5	6	7	8	9	10	11	12	13	14	15	16	17	18
19	19	20	1	2	3	4	5	6	7	8	9	10	11	12	13	14	15	16	17	18	19	20	1	2	3	4	5	6	7	8	9	10	11	12	13	14	15	16	17	18	19
20	20	1	2	3	4	5	6	7	8	9	10	11	12	13	14	15	16	17	18	19	20	1	2	3	4	5	6	7	8	9	10	11	12	13	14	15	16	17	18	19	20

BARGELLO PLACE MATS

I made the first set of these table accessories as gifts for my mentor and friend, Brenda Stengel, and her husband, Gordon. They always provided such wonderful hospitality to me when I was teaching at Brenda's shop, Satin Moon, in Victoria, British Columbia, Canada. First, I gave Brenda and Gordon a set of bargello place mats, kind of as a joke. I guess they liked them better than I had anticipated, because Brenda urged me to write instructions and teach a class to make these place mats. On a later visit I gave them a matching table runner (page 80), which I also incorporated into a pattern and a class. These items are among my favorite designs in the book because they look so pretty on a table no matter what color you choose. They also stitch up quickly and make a perfect gift.

CHOOSING FABRICS

These little quilts use 10 fabrics in one color group, with values ranging from light to dark.

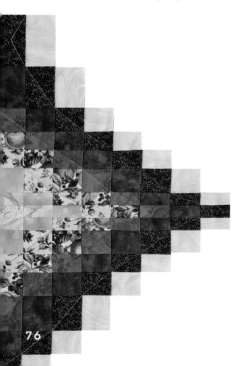

MATERIALS

Yardage is based on 42"-wide fabric. Yields 4 place mats.

¼ yard *each of 10 bargello fabrics**

⅝ yard *of a dark fabric for binding**

1½ yards *of dark fabric for backing*

4 pieces, 17" x 24", of batting

**If you want to make place mats and the coordinating table runner on page 80 from the same fabrics, you'll need ½ yard of each fabric and ⅞ yard total for binding.*

Finished Size: 13" x 19½" ■ Pieced and machine quilted by author

■ CUTTING

From *each* of the 10 bargello fabrics, cut:

3 strips, 1¾" x 42"

From the dark fabric for binding, cut:

8 strips, 2¼" x 42"

■ FABRIC MAP

Referring to page 13, use a scrap of each of your bargello fabrics to create a fabric map. You'll need to refer to your map throughout the project in order to position all of your strips correctly to make the design shown.

■ MAKING THE STRIP-SET TUBES

Three identical tubes of 10 fabrics each will make four place mats.

1. Referring to "Building Strip Sets" on page 14 and using the 1¾"-wide bargello fabric strips, sew the strips together in numerical order according to your fabric map to make three identical strip sets. Press all seam allowances toward the even-number fabrics.

2. Fold each strip set in half lengthwise, right sides together, carefully matching the two long raw edges to make a tube. Make sure the rectangular unit lies flat and straight and that the tube isn't skewed. Sew along the raw edge using a scant ¼"-wide seam allowance. Carefully press the seam allowances toward fabric 10, without pressing any other creases in the unit.

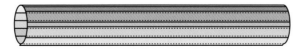

Make 3 tubes.

■ CUTTING THE SLICES

Directions are for making one place mat. Repeat to make a total of four identical place mats.

Place the tube on a cutting mat with a dark fabric at the bottom, closest to your body, and a light fabric at the top of the mat. Refer to "Cutting Slices" on page 16 as needed for guidance. Cut the following slices to make the bargello rows:

Row 1: 1½" wide

Row 2: 1¼" wide

Row 3: 1½" wide

Row 4: 2" wide

Row 5: 1½" wide

Row 6: 1¼" wide

Row 7: 1½" wide

Row 8: 1" wide

Row 9: 1" wide

Row 10: 1" wide

Row 11: 1½" wide

Row 12: 1¼" wide

Row 13: 1¼" wide

Row 14: 1½" wide

Row 15: 2¼" wide

Row 16: 2¾" wide

Row 17: 2¼" wide

Row 18: 1¾" wide

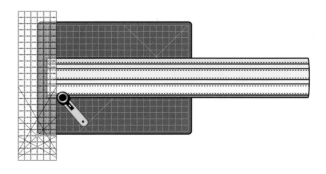

MAKING THE ROWS

Directions are for making one place mat. Repeat to make a total of four identical place mats.

Lay out the slices in the order listed at left to organize the rows for sewing (or you can label the slices with the row number). Turn each fabric loop right side out and remove the stitching between the fabrics as indicated for each row. Refer to the design layout diagram as needed for guidance.

Row 1: Remove the stitching between fabrics 9 and 10.

Rows 2 and 16: Remove the stitching between fabrics 8 and 9.

Rows 3, 15, and 17: Remove the stitching between fabrics 7 and 8.

Rows 4, 14, and 18: Remove the stitching between fabrics 6 and 7.

Rows 5 and 13: Remove the stitching between fabrics 5 and 6.

Rows 6 and 12: Remove the stitching between fabrics 4 and 5.

Rows 7 and 11: Remove the stitching between fabrics 3 and 4.

Rows 8 and 10: Remove the stitching between fabrics 2 and 3.

Row 9: Remove the stitching between fabrics 1 and 2.

JOINING THE ROWS

Directions are for making one place mat. Repeat to make a total of four identical place mats.

1. With right sides together and raw edges aligned, place row 2 on top of row 1. Using a scant ¼"-wide seam allowance, join the rows along their long edges, carefully matching the seam intersections with your finger. You may want to use a stylus or an awl to hold the matched seam intersections in place, gently easing the fabric as needed to align the seams. Press the seam allowances toward row 2.

2. Continue in the same manner, sewing the rows in numerical order and pressing the seam allowances toward the newly added row.

3. Once all the rows are sewn together, finish by basting around the place mat about ⅛" from the outer edges to stabilize the seams for quilting.

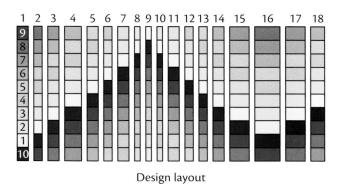

Design layout

FINISHING

1. Layer each place mat with batting and backing. Baste and quilt, referring to pages 92 and 93 as needed. Trim and square up the place mats to measure 13" x 19½".

2. Using the 2¼"-wide binding strips and referring to "Binding" on page 94, make and attach the binding.

QUILTING SUGGESTION

One choice that looks good is to follow the fabric runs up and down across the mat, stitching each rectangle from corner to corner in every other fabric run. To do this, mark the middle of the rectangle where the pattern changes direction with a pencil dot, pivot with your needle down at that point, and then sew in the new direction. Another option is to quilt with an allover meandering pattern.

BARGELLO TABLE RUNNER

This runner coordinates nicely with the place mats on page 76. Once you've made those, you're sure to want to make this table runner too, for a complete dining ensemble.

CHOOSING FABRIC

Select 10 fabrics in one color group with values ranging from light to dark.

MATERIALS

Yardage is based on 42"-wide fabric.

¼ yard each of 10 bargello fabrics

⅓ yard of a dark fabric for binding

1⅔ yards of fabric for backing

24" x 54" piece of batting

CUTTING

From *each* of the 10 bargello fabrics, cut:
3 strips, 1¾" x 42"

From the dark fabric for binding, cut:
4 strips, 2¼" x 42"

FABRIC MAP

Referring to page 13, use a scrap of each of your bargello fabrics to create a fabric map. You'll need to refer to your map throughout the project in order to position all of your strips correctly to make the design shown.

MAKING THE STRIP-SET TUBES

To get the length needed for the table runner, two strip sets are sewn together into a single tube. You'll need two 20-fabric tubes; one will be a full-width (42") tube and the other will be a half-width (21") tube. From these two tubes, you'll be able to cut enough slices for both halves of the table runner.

1. Referring to "Building Strip Sets" on page 14 and using the 1¾"-wide bargello fabric strips, sew the strips together in numerical order according to your fabric map to make three identical strip sets. Press all of the seam allowances toward the even-number fabrics.

Finished Size: 19½" x 49¼" ▪ Pieced and machine quilted by author

2. Join two of the strips sets together, along their long edges, matching fabric 1 on the first strip set to fabric 10 on the second strip set. Press the seam allowances toward fabric 10.

3. Fold the strip set in half lengthwise, right sides together, carefully matching the two remaining long raw edges to make a tube. Make sure the rectangular unit lies flat and straight and that the tube isn't skewed. Sew along the raw edge using a scant 1/4"-wide seam allowance. Carefully press the seam allowances toward fabric 10 without pressing any other creases in the unit.

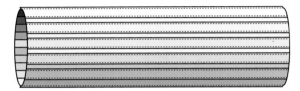

Make 1 full-width tube.

4. Cut the third strip set in half to make two 21"-wide strip units. Repeat steps 2 and 3 to make a half tube, 21" wide.

Make 1 half-width tube.

◼ TOP HALF

The construction of the table runner is similar to the place mats on page 76, except you'll need to make two halves which will be joined in the middle. However, because the table runner is symmetrical, when the two halves are joined, there is a duplicate middle row of fabric rectangles. The rectangles need to be removed from the bottom half to achieve the desired design.

◼ Cutting the Slices

Place a tube on a cutting mat with a dark fabric at the bottom, closest to your body, and a light fabric at the top of the mat. Refer to "Cutting Slices" on page 16 as needed for guidance. Cut the following slices to make the bargello rows for the top half:

Row 1: 2"

Row 2: 2½"

Row 3: 2"

Row 4: 1¾"

Row 5: 1½"

Row 6: 1¼"

Row 7: 1¼"

Row 8: 1"

Row 9: 1"

Row 10: 1"

Row 11: 1¼"

Row 12: 1¼"

Row 13: 1½"

Row 14: 1¾"

Row 15: 2"

Row 16: 2½"

Row 17: 2"

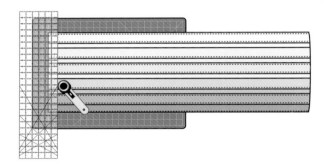

◼ Making the Rows

Lay out the slices in the order listed above to organize the rows for sewing (or you can label the slices with the row number). Turn each fabric loop right side out and remove the stitching between the fabrics as indicated for each row. Refer to the design layout diagram as needed for guidance.

Rows 1 and 17: Remove the stitching between fabrics 9 and 10.

Rows 2 and 16: Remove the stitching between fabrics 8 and 9.

Rows 3 and 15: Remove the stitching between fabrics 7 and 8.

Rows 4 and 14: Remove the stitching between fabrics 6 and 7.

Rows 5 and 13: Remove the stitching between fabrics 5 and 6.

Rows 6 and 12: Remove the stitching between fabrics 4 and 5.

Rows 7 and 11: Remove the stitching between fabrics 3 and 4.

Rows 8 and 10: Remove the stitching between fabrics 2 and 3.

Row 9: Remove the stitching between fabrics 1 and 2.

Row 9 is the middle of the table runner. When all of the fabric loops have been opened at the correct seam, the top half of the table runner should be symmetrical.

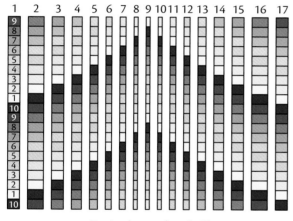

Design layout (top half)

Joining the Rows

1. With right sides together and raw edges aligned, place row 2 on top of row 1. Using a scant ¼"-wide seam allowance, join the rows along their long edges, carefully matching the seam intersections with your finger. You may want to use a stylus or an awl to hold the matched seam intersections in place, gently easing the fabric as needed to align the seams. Press the seam allowances toward row 2.

2. Continue in the same manner, sewing the rows in numerical order and pressing the seam allowances toward the newly added row.

BOTTOM HALF

Following the directions for the top half, cut slices to make the bottom half of the table runner. Before joining the rows, remove the bottom fabric rectangle in each row. Then join the rows together in the same manner as you did for the top half.

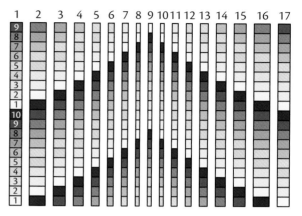

Design layout (bottom half)

ASSEMBLY

1. Turn the bottom half upside down and check to ensure that it's a mirror image of the top half of the table runner. The seam allowances should be going in opposite directions and nest together. Carefully pin the two halves together, matching the seam intersections.

2. Use a scant ¼"-wide seam allowance to stitch the two halves together. Press the seam allowances to one side.

3. Finish by basting around the table runner about ⅛" from the outer edges to stabilize the seams for quilting.

FINISHING

1. Layer the table runner with batting and backing. Baste and quilt, referring to pages 92 and 93 as needed.

2. Using the 2¼"-wide binding strips and referring to "Binding" on page 94, make and attach the binding.

Aurora Borealis by Mary Laanela

Because I love purple, I wanted to try Eileen's first pattern design.

Aurora Borealis by Pat Hunt

Machine quilted by Dianna McCorkall
of Victoria, British Columbia, Canada

Some of my friends had taken Eileen's class at Satin Moon. I didn't take the class but made the quilt anyway and added my own border twist.

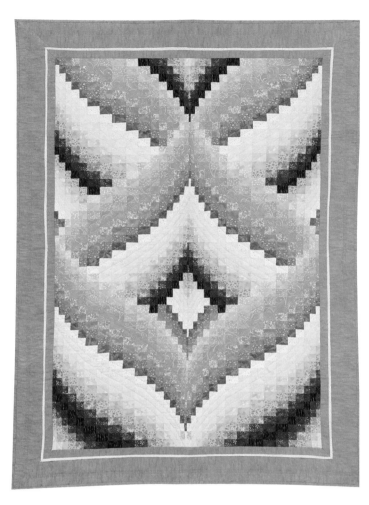

Aurora Borealis by Christina Bell

I started this quilt in Eileen's class at Satin Moon and finished it on my own with totally different colors of my own choosing.

Island Moon by Eileen Wright

This quilt is a second version of the "Island Sunset" design (page 24). This version was made under mental protest using colors requested by my mentor and friend, Brenda Stengel, who owns the shop where I teach. I never buy black fabric unless I absolutely require it and never use sparkly fabrics in my quilts. But Brenda's ongoing support of my work made all this quilting excitement happen in my life so I wanted to comply with her request. This version was very difficult for me to make because I didn't like the fabrics. But when it was finished, I had to agree that it was dramatic and really made a statement. I love this quilt for the learning experience that it was. It totally expanded my mind to the use of other colors—not just my favorites.

Cosmic Twist **by Eileen Wright**

Machine quilted by Nadia Wilson of Port Hardy, British Columbia, Canada

This quilt is a second version of my "Cosmic Twist" design (page 30), which I created as a class sample in a colorway that was new for me. I have since added these colors to my positive list.

Supernova **by Mary Laanela**

Machine quilted by Pat and Don Bays of Nanaimo, British Columbia, Canada

Since Eileen asked me to be one of her official pattern testers, I had some input into the design of this one. I loved the final results of this quilt, so I decided to make it for myself in blue with a hint of purple, which is my favorite color.

Wind Song by Eileen Wright

Machine quilted by Nadia Wilson of Port Hardy, British Columbia, Canada

My conversations with Mary Laanela about her visions for her "Floral Melody" quilt (below) inspired me to make this quilt. As my mind was picturing Mary's idea, it forced me to consider other possibilities for my "Surf Song" design (page 70). The autumn colors with maple leaves blowing in the wind became a very strong image in my head.

Floral Melody by Mary Laanela

I was inspired by Eileen's original "Surf Song" quilt (page 70), but I really wanted to work with floral fabrics. My vision was to create wildflowers rippling in the breeze on a mountain slope.

Christmas Bargello Runner
by Eileen Wright

This runner was made because I could not resist the candy cane fabric on a day when I was teaching a class at Satin Moon. I knew I had a huge collection of other reds and/or Christmas fabrics and it was that time of year.

FINISHING YOUR QUILT

This section provides you with the basic information necessary to finish your quilt. Each of these steps is very important to a beautifully finished quilt that will endure and be treasured for years to come.

BORDERS WITH MITERED CORNERS

When I add borders to my quilts, I always make them multiple borders with mitered corners. Adding a mitered border allows me to create a single border unit of multiple fabrics and then measure, mark, and sew in a single process. Otherwise, the borders could easily be several inches too long and result in wavy or rippling edges. To find the correct length and width measurements for the border strips, you should always measure through the center of the quilt top, not at the outside edges. This will ensure that the borders are of equal length on opposite sides of the quilt and help keep your quilt square.

I like to add a narrow border accent in the seam between the inner and outer borders. For the projects in this book, the border accent always lies toward the outer border, making that border look narrower. However, by placing it this way, the inner border remains 1" wide, replicating the width of the strips in the main part of the quilt. Usually, this is more aesthetically pleasing.

Multiple Border Units

1. To join like border strips, place the strips at right angles, with right sides together. Draw a diagonal line as shown and secure with pins. Stitch on the diagonal line. Trim the excess fabric, leaving a ¼"-wide seam allowance. Press the seam allowances open to reduce bulk and help disguise the seam.

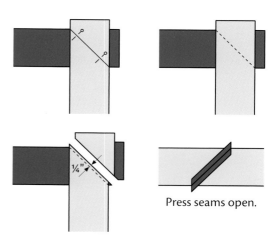

Press seams open.

2. Fold the 1"-wide accent border strip in half lengthwise, *wrong* sides together, and press.

Fold line

3. Align the raw edges of the accent strip with one raw edge of the outer-border strip and machine baste in place with a ⅛"-wide seam allowance. Press the entire length of the border strip to smooth out any puckers.

Raw edges

Machine baste.

4. Lay the inner-border strip on top of the accent strip, right sides together and raw edges aligned. Reset the stitch length, if needed, and sew the inner-border strip to the accent strip with a very straight ¼"-wide seam allowance. Press the seam allowances toward the inner-border strip.

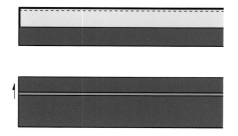

Measuring for Length of Multiple-Border Units

1. Measure the length and width of your quilt top through the center. To each of these measurements add twice the width of your border strip, plus ½" for seam allowances. To be safe, add 3" to 4" to the resulting measurement to give yourself some leeway.

2. Cut two multiple-border units to the measurement for the top and bottom borders. Cut two multiple-border units to the measurement for the side borders.

3. Fold each border unit in half and pin-mark the center. Pin-mark the centers of each side of the quilt top.

4. Lay your quilt top on a large, flat surface, right side facing up, and place the two side border units down the center length of the quilt. The border units should be *wrong* sides up with the inner borders facing each other along the middle row of the quilt top.

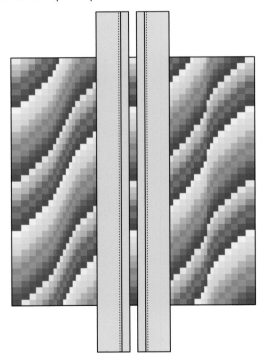

5. In the seam allowance of each border unit, use a pencil or chalk to mark the following positions: the outer edges of the quilt top, ¼" from the outer edge, and 4 to 5 seam lines evenly spaced across the length of the quilt top.

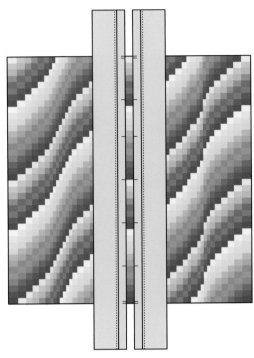

Mark side borders.

6. Repeat steps 4 and 5 to mark the top and bottom border units.

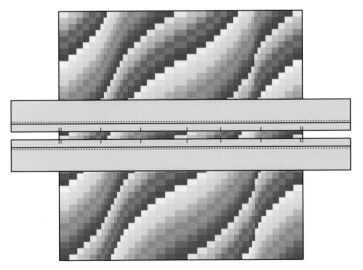

Mark top and bottom borders.

Sewing the Border Units

1. With right sides together, carefully pin the side borders to the quilt, matching the center pins and outer edges. Match the seam lines of the quilt top to the marks on the border units.

2. Sew the strips to the quilt, being careful to start and stop sewing exactly at the ¼" mark. Backstitch at the beginning and end of the seam. Press the seam allowances toward the border strips.

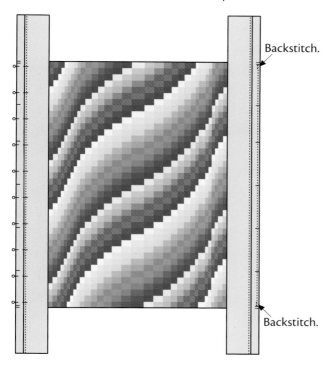

Backstitch.

Backstitch.

3. Repeat steps 1 and 2 for the top and bottom borders.

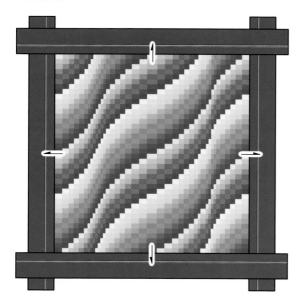

Mitering the Corners

1. Lay your quilt top right side up on a flat surface. Carefully turn down the top border, forming a diagonal fold in the quilt. The raw edges of the two borders should now be aligned, right sides together, and the seam lines of the border units should match.

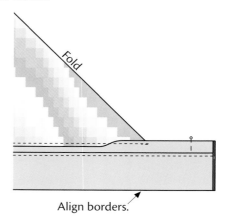

Align borders.

2. Using a ruler marked with a 45° line, align the 45° line on the ruler with the outside edge of the borders and the ruler's edge with the fold. Use a pencil or chalk to draw a line along the edge of the ruler.

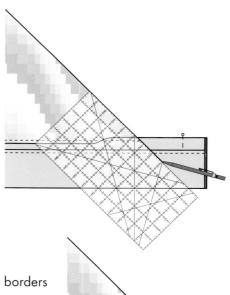

3. Pin the borders together, making sure the seam lines match.

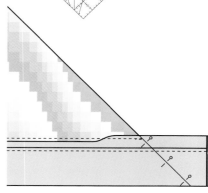

4. Mark and pin the remaining three corners in the same manner before sewing.

5. Sew on the drawn line, beginning at the inside corner and backstitching at the beginning and end of the seam. (Make sure the border seam allowance does not get caught in the mitered seam.) Sew the remaining three corners in the same manner.

6. Open the quilt and look at the front, making sure that the seam lines match and that the seam lies flat. When you are satisfied that everything looks good, cut away the extra border fabric, leaving a ¼"-wide seam allowance. Press the seam allowances open.

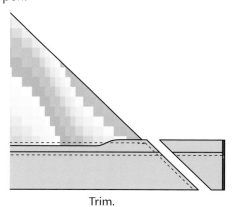

Trim.

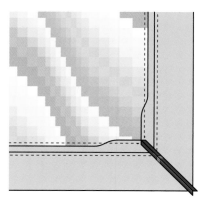

Press seam open.

■ LAYERING AND BASTING

When your quilt top is complete, measure the width and length. You will need batting and backing pieces that are at least 4" larger on all sides than your quilt top. If you plan to have your project quilted by a professional machine quilter, check with that person before preparing your finished quilt top and backing in any way.

Measure and cut the fabric into the number of lengths needed; then sew the lengths together using a 1"-wide seam allowance. Trim off the selvages, leaving a ½"-wide seam allowance. Press the seam allowances open to reduce bulk. (You can also use extra-wide backing fabric so your backing can be cut in one piece. Extra-wide backings can range from 60" wide to 120" wide.) Trim the backing to the required size.

If you plan to machine quilt your project, pin basting is an easy and efficient way to baste the quilt sandwich. Before you layer the quilt, press the backing and the entire quilt top, correcting any errant seam allowances from the wrong side. The quilt should lie flat, smooth, and square.

1. Lay the backing, wrong side facing up, on a clean, flat surface (a table works well). Anchor the backing with masking tape, making sure that it is straight and square. The backing should be smooth and taut, but not stretched so tightly that the fabric becomes distorted.

2. Lay the batting over the backing, and then center the quilt top, right side facing up, over the batting. Make sure there are no wrinkles in any layer and that the batting and quilt top are parallel to the edges of the backing.

3. Using No. 2 rustproof safety pins, place pins over the surface of the quilt, about 3" apart. Plan the placement so that the pins are not in the way of the quilting lines. Pin in two stages. First, insert the safety pins and leave them open. When the entire top is basted, first remove the tape, and then close the pins. With less tension on the fabric the pins will be easier to close.

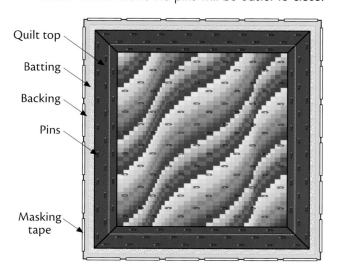

Quilt top
Batting
Backing
Pins
Masking tape

MACHINE QUILTING

Machine quilting is suitable for all types of quilts. With machine quilting, you can quickly complete one project and move on to the next.

If machine quilting always stumps you, you are not alone. Personally, my joy is in the piecing. If you want to quilt your project on your home sewing machine, I urge you to take classes from those teachers whose work you admire. There are also many excellent books available to guide you through machine quilting. For more information on machine quilting, refer to *Machine Quilting Made Easy!* by Maurine Noble (Martingale & Company, 1994).

If you prefer to have the quilting done by a professional, ask at your local quilt shop for references about someone in your area who does this type of work.

SQUARING UP YOUR QUILT

When you complete the quilting, you'll need to trim the excess backing and batting as well as square up your quilt before attaching the binding. Make sure all the basting pins have been removed. Position a ruler along the seam line of the inner border (or a bargello row) and trim the excess batting and backing from all four sides. Use a square ruler to square up each corner to a true 90° angle.

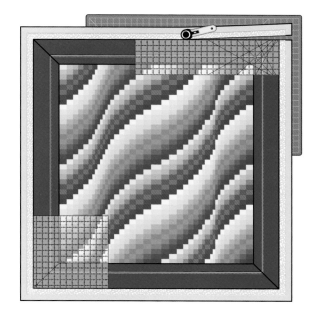

ADDING A HANGING SLEEVE

If you plan to hang the finished quilt, attach a hanging sleeve or rod pocket to the back now, before you bind the quilt.

1. Cut a 7"-wide strip of fabric long enough to span the width of your quilt, plus about 3". On each short end, fold over 1", and then fold over 1" again. Press and topstitch by machine.

2. Fold the fabric in half lengthwise, wrong sides together, and press. Pin the sleeve in place on the back of the quilt, matching the raw edges of the sleeve with the raw edges of the quilt sandwich. The quilt should be about ½" wider than the sleeve on both ends. Machine baste the top edge of the sleeve in place using a ⅛"-wide seam allowance. (The raw edges and seam will be covered when you sew on the binding.)

Baste sleeve to top edge.

3. Finish the sleeve after the binding has been attached by hand stitching the bottom of the sleeve in place, after pushing the bottom edge of the sleeve up just a bit to accommodate the hanging rod.

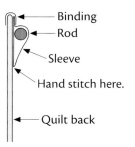

BINDING

I recommend straight-grain double-fold binding. All the bindings for the quilts in this book were cut 2¼" wide across the width of fabric and then pieced.

1. To make one long, continuous strip, sew the strips, right sides together, at right angles, stitching across the corner as shown. Trim the seam allowances to ¼" and press them open.

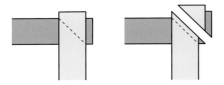

2. Fold the strip in half lengthwise, wrong sides together, and press.

Fold line

3. Starting on one side of the quilt, not at a corner, match the raw edge of the binding with the raw edge of the quilt. Leaving about an 8" tail of binding, start sewing using a ¼"-wide seam allowance. Stop sewing ¼" from the corner; backstitch and remove the quilt from the machine.

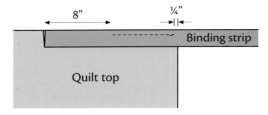

4. Turn the quilt so you will be ready to sew the next edge. First, fold the binding up and away from the quilt so the fold forms a 45° angle. Then fold the binding back down onto itself, even with the edge of the quilt top. The fold should be aligned with the corner of the quilt top. Begin with a backstitch

at the fold of the binding and continue stitching along the edge of the quilt top, mitering each corner as you come to it.

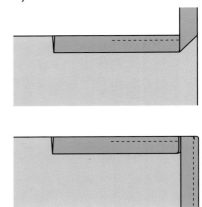

5. Stop stitching about 8" from the starting end of the binding strip and backstitch. Remove the quilt from the machine.

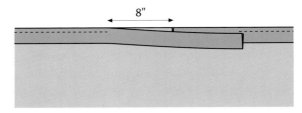

6. Place the quilt on a flat surface and overlap the beginning and ending tails of the binding. On the beginning tail, insert a pin in the fold of the binding about 3" from the end of the binding strip. Insert a second pin in the same position on the ending tail as shown. (This is the center point where the diagonal seam will cross the two tails.)

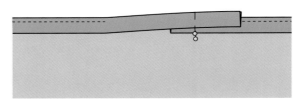

7. Unfold both ends of the binding. Open and lay the ending tail right side up. Open and lay the beginning tail over it, right side down, matching the two pin points with another pin inserted through both tails. Pin the ends together and carefully draw a diagonal line between the points where the strips intersect, through the pin point.

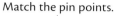

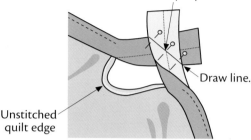

Match the pin points.

Draw line.

Unstitched quilt edge

8. Sew the binding ends together along the drawn line. Trim the excess fabric, leaving a ¼"-wide seam allowance. Finger-press the seam allowances open; then refold the binding strip and sew it in place on the quilt.

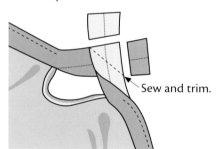

Sew and trim.

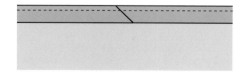

Complete stitching.

9. Fold the binding to the back of the quilt so that it covers the machine stitching. Hand stitch in place, folding the miters as you reach each corner.

Fold first.

Fold second.

Quilt back

SIGNING YOUR FINISHED QUILT

Remember to add a label to your quilt for posterity. At a minimum, the label should include the title of the quilt, the name of the quiltmaker, where the quilt was made, and the date of completion. Additional information may include the inspiration or name of the designer. You may also want to include the special reason you made the quilt, and if the quilt is a gift, include the name of the recipient and any other significant facts about the quilt. Use a permanent pen or marker to write on your labels or make them on your computer and print them out on fabric sheets. Hand stitch your label to a lower corner of the quilt backing.

SURF SONG

Designed and made by Eileen Wright Nanaimo, B.C. November 2008

Care Label

Sometimes it is a good idea to include a typed "Care Information" sheet with a gift quilt so the recipient knows how to care for such a special gift.

ABOUT THE AUTHOR

A sewer and a knitter since she was eight years old, Eileen Wright has always worked creatively with needles and threads of some kind, working her way through most needlecraft hobbies over the years. She feels indebted to her maternal grandmother, Cynthia Rassmussen, for passing on her talents and love of being creative.

Vancouver Island in Canada has been Eileen's spiritual home since her very first visit, and she feels fortunate to have been able to live there for almost 20 years. She fills her days with designing and creating quilts.

Eileen shares her condo with three Pfaff sewing machines, a huge fabric stash, and some green growing plants—all of which provide her with all the serenity she craves. Huge skylights allow the sun to shine on her workspace, and an ever-changing view of the ocean and distant mountains often inspires various quilting projects. Eileen loves that no one ever interrupts her by asking "What's for dinner?" and happily states that life just couldn't be any better than this.